Testimonies of Trauma, Trials, & Triumphs

My Personal Path of Healing

By Jody LaTampa

Table of Contents

Dedication   1

Prayer   3

Foreword   5

Publisher's Foreword   7

Healing, Miracles, Redemption, and Transformation   9

My Genesis   19

Superman   33

Kryptonite   45

Redemption   65

Trials Just Like Job   73

A Revolution Begins   81

Jesus My King   91

Superman's Demise   99

Grief   113

A Pandemic   133

Forgiveness and the Return to My Call   143

Purpose   159

Healing   177

The Pardon   189

My Gift from God "Nathaniel"   221

Similitude   237

Legacy   253

Triumphs   261

Testimonies: We All Have Faces   275

Jody's Art Gallery of Healing   281

Dedication

To Jesus, the foundation of my faith and the source of unwavering strength, I offer my deepest gratitude. Your love and guidance have been a constant presence in my life, guiding me through every twist and turn.

To my son, Nathaniel, you are a precious gift from above, and your presence in my life has brought immeasurable joy and purpose. Your love, laughter, and boundless enthusiasm have been a light in my darkest moments.

To my beloved parents, your unwavering support and belief in me has shaped who I am today. You have been my pillars of strength, and I am forever grateful for your endless love.

To my best friend, your friendship has been a source of comfort and joy in every season of my life. Your presence has been a blessing beyond measure.

To my mentors, you have shared your wisdom and knowledge, pushing me to grow and reach new heights. Your guidance has been invaluable, and I am indebted to you.

To my family of faith, you have been a source of inspiration and encouragement, standing beside me in times of change and uncertainty.

To my beloved late husband Kenny, from the depths of my heart, I offer this dedication to you. Through our trials and triumphs, I have come to know the true depth of God's love and the profound healing it brings. Without you, I would have never truly understood what lies within me.

The loss of your physical presence in my life has been a profound challenge. Your absence has taught me the value of cherishing every moment, and your memory continues to inspire me to live each day to the fullest.

As I navigate this path without you, I hold on to the cherished memories we created together. I promise to honor your memory by living a life filled with love, kindness, and compassion. Thank you, Kenny, for the love you bestowed upon me and for the profound impact you had on my life.

This book is dedicated to each of you for your love, support, and encouragement. You have all played an integral part in this journey, and I am eternally grateful.

May the wisdom and knowledge within these pages guide others on a journey of self-discovery and spiritual growth. May the healing process begin within them. Bless their time with this book, that it may illuminate their path and bring them into a deeper understanding of Your grace and healing power.

Prayer

———◆❖◆———

Gracious God, as others open the pages of this co-authored book, I come before you and pray that with open hearts, minds, ears, and eyes, they seek understanding and healing through the words inspired by your divine wisdom and holy scripture. I am honored that it was co-created by you and me. May everyone who encounters this work be touched by its message and recognize the presence of your love and inspiration throughout. Grant me the humility to acknowledge that I am merely an instrument of your divine plan, and may this book serve as a vessel to spread your grace and teachings to all who read it.

I decree and declare over the readers that the pain they may feel today be the greatest testimony they will tell! The hurt they experience will help be the strength they will wield! The problems they face today will be the source of their prosperity! Nothing they go through today will be wasted tomorrow!

I recognize that You, God, are the ultimate source of truth and healing, and I pray that this book serves as a conduit for your guidance and love to flow into their hearts. May it lead them closer to your eternal truth and the profound healing only you can provide. In Your precious name, Jesus, I pray. Amen.

Foreword

In the pages of *Trauma, Trials, Testimonies, and Triumphs*, I invite you to embark on an extraordinary journey—one that celebrates the resilience of the human spirit and the transformative power of embracing life's struggles. As the author of this book, I will share with you that you should stop trying to skip the struggle, for it is here "in the struggle" where your character is truly built.

In a world that often glorifies instant success and seeks shortcuts to happiness, it's easy to forget the profound truth: character is built in the crucible of hardship. Life's trials become our teachers, guiding us toward a deeper understanding of ourselves and others. Through the personal testimonies shared within these pages, you will witness the raw, unfiltered experiences of those who have faced adversity head-on, demonstrating the unwavering spirit that emerges when you confront your challenges and shortcomings with Jesus, courage, and determination.

Together, we will learn the art of embracing struggle—the art of facing your fears, your doubts, and your pain with unwavering resolve. In doing so, you will unearth a wellspring of inner strength that empowers you to rise above circumstances and rewrite your own stories of triumph.

By the end of this journey, you will have witnessed firsthand how ordinary people like me can turn their struggles into sources of inspiration, hope, and resilience. The stories will resonate with you, reminding you that you, too, have the power to overcome anything life throws your way.

So, dear reader, let us embark on this shared odyssey. Let us embrace the struggles, learn from them, and, in doing so, grow into the best version of ourselves. Together, we shall discover the indomitable strength that lies within each one of us and embrace the fullness of life's experiences. Through it all, let us find comfort in the knowledge that Jesus walks with you, ensuring that you never have to face these trials alone.

Let this book be a guiding light, illuminating the path to your self-discovery and reminding us all that in the face of adversity, your true character shines brightly—forever unyielding, forever triumphant.

With profound sincerity, Jody LaTampa

(*Author of Testimonies of Trauma, Trials and Triumphs*)

Publisher's Foreword

What a privilege and honor it is to be the publisher of Testimonies of Trauma, Trials, and Triumphs. When I started ChosenButterfly Publishing in 2013, the Lord gave me the tagline "We Publish Books that Transform Lives," and I believe this book fully captures that vision.

Years ago, I was deeply moved by Jody's profound and anointed Facebook posts. I couldn't help but reach out to her and say, "Write a book, and I will publish it!" I knew she had a powerful message that could be a blessing to the masses, and I wanted to provide her thoughts with a platform to touch as many people as possible. It took a few years, but it has finally happened! The book you are holding in your hands today is beyond what even I had envisioned.

The healing that is locked within these pages is unleashed upon reading. Even the editor couldn't help but shed tears and couldn't say enough about how this book touched, moved, and healed her as she worked on it. This book has been a labor of love, prayer, and faith, and I believe it is saturated with blessings.

I know Jody and many others in her life have prayed earnestly about this book and for you, the reader. I, too, join my faith and prayer with theirs and say, "May the Lord Jesus speak to you through these pages, may healing and deliverance come into your life, and when you are done reading this book, may you experience the love of Jesus at another level."

Testimonies of Trauma, Trials, and Triumphs is a testament to the enduring power of faith, hope, and the healing grace of God. It's a book that will inspire, uplift, and offer solace to those in need. As a publisher, I couldn't be more grateful to have been part of bringing this incredible story to light, and I believe this book has the potential to transform lives, just as we set out to do from the very beginning. Enjoy the journey, and may you find hope, healing, and a deeper connection with Jesus, our Lord and Savior, within these pages.

Love and Blessings,

Ayanna Lynnay

Founder of ChosenButterfly Publishing

www.cb-publishing.com

Healing, Miracles, Redemption, and Transformation

Jeremiah 17:14

Heal me, Lord, and I will be healed, save me, and I will be saved,
for you are my praise.

This is my story, a journey of profound healing through the boundless love of Jesus, guided by the empowering embrace of Grace. As I traversed the rocky terrains of life, burdened by pain and darkness, I found healings, miracles, redemption, and transformation in the divine presence, a beacon of hope that illuminated my path.

In my seasons of despair, I learned to seek refuge in prayer, pouring my heart out to the one who listens without judgment. Through every tear I shed, I felt a gentle hand lifting me, whispering words of comfort and reassurance. With each step, the weight of my burdens lightened, as I surrendered my worries to the unwavering faith in God's plan.

Grace became my constant companion, gently nudging me towards forgiveness and self-compassion. It embraced my flaws, reminding me that I am loved unconditionally. It taught me to let go of past hurts, opening doors to newfound freedom and self-discovery.

In Jesus, I discovered a love so unconditional and powerful that it healed wounds I thought were irreparable. His teachings freed my soul, showing me the path to redemption and inner peace.

This journey wasn't without challenges. There were moments when doubt tried to creep in, and shadows threatened to overpower the light. Yet, with unwavering faith and the grace-filled strength that enveloped me, I overcame and persevered with the help of Jesus.

As I look back on my story, I am humbled by the undeniable power of Jesus Christ. This undoubtedly turned my brokenness into resilience, my pain into purpose, my mess into a message, my test into testimonies, and all of my doubts into unrelenting faith.

May my journey inspire others to embrace their own healing with open hearts, for within the arms of Jesus and the sanctuary of Grace, miracles await, and a life of wholeness unfolds.

For those who may be new believers, I am eager to share some fundamental teachings and terminologies related to my spiritual journey, which you will find throughout this book. The following chapter has essential insights that have enriched my understanding of faith and guided me in my own path of belief.

As we embark on this exploration together, may these teachings serve as a source of inspiration and guidance, fostering a deeper connection with understanding.

First, let me discuss In the biblical context, healing and miracles, how they are closely related but distinctly different concepts.

Healing refers to the restoration of health or wholeness in an individual, which could be physical, emotional, or spiritual. It often involves the recovery from illness, disease, or any affliction that causes suffering.

Miracles, on the other hand, are extraordinary events that transcend the natural order and are attributed to divine intervention or supernatural power. Miracles can include various acts, such as healing the sick, raising the dead, walking on water, and multiplying food, among many others.

In the Bible, Jesus performed numerous miracles, and many of them involved healing the sick or disabled. These were seen as signs of His divine nature and were meant to demonstrate God's power, love, and compassion for humanity. They also served to strengthen people's faith and belief in God's ability to intervene in their lives.

Here's a list of seven healings performed by Jesus, along with the corresponding scripture references:

1. *Healing the leper - Matthew 8:1-4*

"When Jesus came down from the mountainside, large crowds followed him. A man with leprosy came and knelt before him and said, 'Lord, if you are willing, you can make me clean.' Jesus reached out his hand and touched the man. 'I am willing,' he said. 'Be clean!' Immediately, he was cleansed of his leprosy. Then Jesus said to him, 'See that you don't tell anyone. But go, show yourself to the priest and offer the gift Moses commanded, as a testimony to them.'"

2. *Healing the centurion's servant - Matthew 8:5-13*

"When Jesus had entered Capernaum, a centurion came to him, asking for help. 'Lord,' he said, 'my servant lies at home paralyzed, suffering terribly.' Jesus said to him, 'Shall I come and heal him?' The centurion replied, 'Lord, I do not deserve to have you come under my roof. But just say the word, and my servant will be healed...'"

3. *Healing the paralyzed man - Matthew 9:1-8*

"Jesus stepped into a boat, crossed over and came to his own town. Some men brought to him a paralyzed man, lying on a mat. When Jesus saw their faith, he said to the man, 'Take heart, son; your sins are forgiven.' At this, some of the teachers of the law said to themselves, 'This fellow is blaspheming!'"

4. *Healing the woman with the issue of blood - Matthew 9:20-22*

"Just then, a woman who had been subject to bleeding for twelve years came up behind him and touched the edge of his cloak. She said to herself, 'If I only touch his cloak, I will be healed.' Jesus turned and saw her. 'Take heart, daughter,' he said, 'your faith has healed you.' And the woman was healed at that moment."

5. *Healing the blind men - Matthew 9:27-31*

"As Jesus went on from there, two blind men followed him, calling out, 'Have mercy on us, Son of David!' When he had gone indoors, the blind men came to him, and he asked them, 'Do you believe that I am able to do this?' 'Yes, Lord,' they replied. Then he touched their eyes and said, 'According to your faith, let it be done to you'; and their sight was restored."

6. *Healing the man with a withered hand - Matthew 12:9-14*

"Going on from that place, he went into their synagogue, and a man with a shriveled hand was there. Looking for a reason to bring charges against Jesus, they asked him, 'Is it lawful to heal on the Sabbath?' He said to them, 'If any of you has a sheep and it falls into a pit on the Sabbath, will you not take hold of it and lift it out? How much more valuable is a person than a sheep!'"

7. Healing the blind and mute demon-possessed man - Matthew 12:22-23

"Then they brought him a demon-possessed man who was blind and mute, and Jesus healed him, so that he could both talk and see. All the people were astonished and said, 'Could this be the Son of David?'"

These accounts can be found in the New Testament, specifically in the Gospel of Matthew.

Here are five miracles performed by God and Jesus, along with their corresponding scriptures:

1. Miracle of Creation (God's Miracle) - Genesis 1:1-31

"In the beginning, God created the heavens and the earth..."

2. Parting of the Red Sea (God's Miracle) - Exodus 14:21-22

"Then Moses stretched out his hand over the sea, and the Lord drove the sea back by a strong east wind all night and made the sea dry land, and the waters were divided."

3. Feeding of the 5,000 (Jesus' Miracle) - Matthew 14:19-21

"Then he ordered the crowds to sit down on the grass, and taking the five loaves and the two fish, he looked up to heaven and said a blessing. Then he broke the loaves and gave them to the disciples, and the disciples gave them to the crowds."

4. Healing of Mary Magdalene (Jesus' Miracle)-Luke 8:1-2:

"After this, Jesus traveled about from one town and village to another, proclaiming the good news of the kingdom of God. The Twelve were with him, and also some women who had been cured of evil spirits and diseases: Mary (called Magdalene) from whom seven demons had come out."

5. *Jesus' Resurrection (Jesus' Miracle) - Matthew 28:5-6*

"But the angel said to the women, 'Do not be afraid, for I know that you seek Jesus who was crucified. He is not here, for he has risen, as he said.'"

These are just some of the miracles that demonstrate the divine power and intervention of God and Jesus in the Bible.

Jesus is found in John 14:12 where he says, "Very truly I tell you, whoever believes in me will do the works I have been doing, and they will do even greater things than these because I am going to the Father."

This verse suggests that believers who have faith in Jesus will have the capacity to perform healings and miraculous acts of service similar to those Jesus did during his earthly ministry, and even greater ones, after his ascension to heaven.

Faith is the complete trust and confidence in God's promises and His existence, even when it is unseen or unknown. It involves believing in His character, His Word, and His ability to fulfill what He has said.

Key scriptures that describe faith:

Hebrews 11:1: "Now faith is the assurance of things hoped for, the conviction of things not seen." This verse emphasizes that faith involves a deep conviction and assurance in things that are yet to be realized or physically observed.

Another notable passage on faith is found in:

Hebrews 11:6: "And without faith, it is impossible to please him, for whoever would draw near to God must believe that he exists and that he rewards those who seek him."

This verse highlights the significance of faith in our relationship with God and the importance of believing in His existence and His willingness to reward those who seek Him diligently.

The entire chapter of Hebrews 11 serves as a great example of various individuals throughout history who demonstrated faith in God and were commended for it. From Abel and Enoch to Abraham and Moses, these individuals exhibited unwavering trust in God's promises, even in the face of challenges and uncertainties.

In summary, biblical faith is a firm belief and trust in God, His Word, and His promises, even when we cannot see or fully comprehend His plan. It is essential for our relationship with God and is exemplified by the lives of those who have gone before us.

His ways are not our ways. He works in both the seen and the unseen, the tested and the unproven. There are many ways you can expect God to heal you and others. The first place you start is with prayer and faith, and then His healing will come. The seven ways I have listed here come from my studies, but do not put limits on God. He wants to heal all of his creation, and He will do it in His way and in His time.

Here are just seven biblical ways to healing as demonstrated in the Bible, along with their corresponding scriptures:

1. Prayer and Faith:

The Bible emphasizes the power of prayer and faith in God's ability to bring healing. James 5:15 says, "And the prayer of faith will save the one who is sick, and the Lord will raise him up."

2. Anointing with Oil:

In James 5:14, it is written, "Is anyone among you sick? Let them call the elders of the church to pray over them and anoint them with oil in the name of the Lord."

3. God's Word:

Psalm 107:20 states, "He sent out his word and healed them, and delivered them from their destruction."

4. Repentance and Forgiveness:

Healing is often linked to repentance and forgiveness. James 5:16 encourages, "Confess your sins to one another and pray for one another, that you may be healed."

5. Laying on of Hands:

In Mark 16:18, Jesus said, "They will lay hands on the sick, and they will recover."

6. Deliverance:

Deliverance refers to being set free or rescued from bondage, oppression, or any form of captivity. Psalm 34:17 says, "The righteous cry out, and the Lord hears them; he delivers them from all their troubles."

7. God's Grace and Sovereignty:

Ultimately, healing is in God's hands, and His grace can bring about miraculous recoveries. 2 Corinthians 12:9 says, "My grace is sufficient for you, for my power is made perfect in weakness."

These biblical ways of healing demonstrate the loving and compassionate nature of God, who cares for His people and desires their well-being. While healing may not always happen in the ways we expect or in our timeline, trusting in God's wisdom and sovereignty can bring comfort and hope during times of illness or hardship.

Along with healing and miracles, there is much to be said about redemption and transformation.

In a biblical context, redemption refers to the act of being saved or delivered from sin and its consequences through the sacrifice of Jesus Christ. It is the process of regaining one's spiritual freedom and reconciliation with God.

Transformation, on the other hand, refers to the profound change that occurs in an individual's life when they accept Christ's redemption. It involves a renewing of the mind and character, turning away from sinful behavior, and adopting godly virtues.

Corresponding scriptures:

1. *Redemption:*

Ephesians 1:7 - "In him, we have redemption through his blood, the forgiveness of our trespasses, according to the riches of his grace."

2. *Transformation:*

Romans 12:2 - "Do not be conformed to this world, but be transformed by the renewal of your mind, that by testing you may discern what is the will of God, what is good and acceptable and perfect."

2 Corinthians 5:17 - "Therefore, if anyone is in Christ, he is a new creation. The old has passed away; behold, the new has come."

These scriptures emphasize the significance of redemption through Christ's sacrifice and the subsequent transformation that occurs in the life of a believer.

In the course of our discussion, I have shared the timeless teachings of Jesus, which have undoubtedly left a profound impact on humanity, inspiring countless individuals to seek miracles, healing, redemption, and transformation.

Now, as I embark on sharing my own journey, I pray my story will add a unique and personal dimension to these enduring principles. By opening up about my trauma, trials, testimonies, and triumphs, I hope it will open your eyes to the power of Jesus and you see God in action, demonstrating how he has guided me through moments of struggle, nurtured healing in my life, and led me towards profound transformation.

I pray my story becomes an inspiration, highlighting the potential for growth and renewal that lies within each of us. As I continue to share my journey, may it serve as a source of encouragement and strength for others, advancing a deeper understanding of the timeless wisdom that has touched countless lives throughout history.

My Genesis

John 1:1

In the beginning, there was the word.

In the beginning, there was me. Four and a half years later, there was a little blonde-haired, blue-eyed boy. My brother. We lived in a middle-class area in a middle-class home. My father was an engineer for aircraft braking systems. He was also a volunteer firefighter and an EMT. Inspired by his experience and the desire to protect his community further, my dad decided to take a step beyond firefighting. He realized that serving as a councilman would provide him with an opportunity to influence policies and make a lasting impact on the village he grew up in.

Over the years, my father's dedication and commitment to public service only grew stronger. His genuine desire to improve the lives of others led him to become the mayor of our small village. As the mayor, he brought innovative ideas, compassion, and a strong sense of integrity to his leadership. His impact continues to resonate within the village and in the hearts of those he touched.

My father's exemplary community involvement and strong work ethic have had a profound influence on shaping the person I am today. Witnessing his selflessness and dedication in giving back to the community inspired me to become actively involved in various social causes. His commitment to excellence in his professional endeavors taught me the importance of hard work, perseverance, and integrity in achieving success. Through his compassionate actions and unwavering principles, he instilled in me the values of empathy, communication skills, kindness, and the desire to make a positive difference in the lives of others.

His guidance and support have been instrumental in nurturing my passion for community service and fueling my drive to excel in my own career. I am deeply grateful for the invaluable life lessons he imparted, and I will continue to honor his legacy by following in his footsteps and contributing positively to the world around me.

My mother gave her life to raising my brother and me, and in addition to her nurturing qualities, she instilled the spirit of excellence in me. She emphasized the importance of doing your best, setting high standards, and striving for mastery in all aspects of life. My mother possesses many admirable qualities that have undoubtedly influenced me positively. Her guidance shaped my character and instilled valuable traits in me. For example, although silly, she reminded me of the importance of making my bed in the morning. It symbolized the significance of discipline and attention to detail in my daily life.

By mastering such small tasks, I learned the foundation of taking on greater challenges. With my mother's influence and my willingness to embrace these lessons, I have learned I can take on the world with confidence and resilience.

She was right. How could I ever conquer the world if I couldn't even make my bed in the morning?

I had my season of rebellion as a teenager and young adult, but that is for another time and place.

My father and mother's guidance and encouragement inspired determination, follow through, empathy, perseverance, and responsibility.

Throughout the early stages of my life, I am deeply grateful for the unwavering guidance provided by my parents. Their instruction has been instrumental in shaping the person I am today. From the very beginning, they nurtured my curiosity, encouraged my interests, and instilled in me a sense of responsibility and compassion.

Their dedication to my development has laid a strong foundation for my journey, and I am forever thankful for the invaluable life lessons they bestowed upon me. Their constant presence and belief in my potential has been a true blessing, and I will always cherish the role they played in shaping my character and aspirations.

At the age of twenty-five, I embraced the journey of marriage. However, my husband and I encountered challenges early on while trying to conceive. For three long years, we attempted to have a baby without success. Faced with this difficult situation, we made the brave decision to explore doctors and then ultimately fertility treatments. I was ecstatic when I became pregnant within the first month of use.

With hope, we embarked on this path, and eventually, our dreams were realized as we welcomed our precious baby boy "Nathaniel" which biblically means a gift from God, into our lives. The journey was filled with both ups, downs, and many doctor and hospital visits, but the arrival of our child three weeks early brought immeasurable joy to my life.

But my life took a sharp turn as I faced the devastating discovery of some of my husband's indiscretions. Discovering this, I felt a range of intense emotions. Emotions of shock, disbelief, and a sense of numbness. As reality set in, I felt hurt, betrayed, and, to be honest, just pure devastation. A profound sense of sadness and loss of trust overwhelmed me.

Additionally, I began having feelings of inadequacy and self-doubt. I didn't feel I had any worth. I felt unattractive and insecure. I began comparing myself to others and became socially withdrawn. It had a negative impact on my overall self-confidence. But I still, at times, had a desire to salvage the marriage.

We attempted to rebuild what was lost. Despite our efforts, the wounds were too deep, and the pain from the betrayal lingered in me. It left me with a heavy heart and soon I filed for a divorce with my three-year-old son towing my side.

In my small trailer, which was all I could afford at the time, I began to find comfort in prayer and watching church on TV. One day, I was overwhelmed by a sense of uncertainty about my future. After laying my son Nathaniel down for a nap, I sank into the couch, lost in contemplation. As fatigue and my thoughts took over, I slipped into sleep.

Suddenly, a loud and boisterous voice pierced through my ears, shaking me awake. "Jody, get up!" the voice commanded, thundering through my mind. My heart raced as I struggled to comprehend what was happening. Once more, the voice resounded, urgency filling the air like a loud trumpet. "Jody, get up!" This time, I stirred on the couch, my senses slowly returning to reality.

A peculiar scent began to creep into my awareness, mingling with the remnants of my dreams. It was the unmistakable odor of gas, sharp and alarming. The fog of sleep lifted abruptly as my survival instincts kicked in. Adrenaline surged through me, dispelling my drowsiness. Swiftly, I got up from the couch, my heart still pounding from the startling experience.

Realizing that this encounter was unlike anything I'd ever experienced before, I couldn't shake the feeling that it was an encounter with the voice of God. The urgency of the voice, the abrupt awakening, and the subsequent realization that something was amiss all pointed to a divine intervention.

Reacting quickly, I ran and grabbed Nathaniel from his crib, holding him close as a rush of emotions and relief washed over me. As I moved through the trailer, the scent of gas grew stronger, and it became clear that there was a gas leak. In a panic, I ran outside, and I immediately called the fire department. When they arrived, they confirmed my worst fears—my son and I had been in grave danger. The gas leak could have led to a carbon monoxide buildup, and the consequences could have been fatal.

The gravity of the situation hit me like a ton of bricks. It was a chilling reminder of how fragile life can be and how significant it is to heed the signs around us. The audible voice that protected me and my son during that gas leak became an undeniable sign, a direct communication from something greater than myself. This tangible encounter defied any rational explanation and stood as a powerful testament to the existence of a guiding presence that watched over us in times of peril. It was a deeply personal connection that reaffirmed my faith and solidified the belief that there was a divine plan at play, even when life's path seemed uncertain.

It was during this period of profound revelation that my maternal grandmother, who had been widowed for over thirty years, helped navigate me into the arms of a savior that I truly didn't know. She would call in the evening after I had tucked Nathaniel into bed for the night. She would often say to me, "Jody, my eyesight is diminishing. Could you read the book of John or how about Psalms?"

Although at the age of nine, I had attended vacation bible school with a neighbor, recited the sinners' prayer, and received salvation, I always found myself lacking in wisdom, knowledge, and understanding of the true depth of biblical teachings.

While I had taken the first step towards faith, my journey into a profound understanding of the scriptures was just beginning with my grandmother.

This ongoing pursuit of weekly telephone conversations had a transformative process, shaping my beliefs and strengthening my faith in remarkable ways.

As a child, I had a special bond with my spirit-filled grandmother, who always encouraged me to read my Bible regularly. Though I loved her deeply, I was a rebellious teen. Sometimes she would visit from out of state. I often would put little notes in her baggage. When she arrived back home, she would call and thank me for her letter, asking me if I had read my Bible. I would tell her yes. Which, by the way, was absolutely not the truth. I still have a deep-seated conviction about those little white lies I told her.

I did not realize the sweet secret my grandmother held until many years later, the secret that was revealed when she asked me to read the Bible to her in those late evening phone conversations. Unbeknownst to me, my grandmother would leave twenty-dollar bills tucked within the pages of my Bible on every visit she made to Ohio. Her actions were a testament to her love and faith in me, even when I fell short. Looking back, I'm touched by her thoughtfulness and her understanding of my youthful journey with spirituality.

Her unwavering support and those hidden surprises taught me valuable lessons about honesty, love, and the profound impact of small acts of kindness. Tucked between the Bible's pages, I discovered over one hundred dollars. At that time, I was a struggling single mom, trying to make ends meet. The unexpected windfall felt like a miracle. The seeds she had sown held the promise of buying diapers and providing the food we so desperately needed. It was a reminder that sometimes, help arrives in the most unexpected ways. I consider the significance that Jesus and faith held in my grandmother's life. I finally understood her perspective, and it made me appreciate Jesus and the value it brought to her during her own difficult times.

In the wake of my devastating divorce, a profound transformation occurred within me. It was during this time that the love I had discovered for Jesus grew deeper and became the foundation of my life.

I began to attend church. One evening, I felt a strong call to the altar after the pastor invited anyone in need of prayer. I walked to the altar, something I had never done. But something in me, a gentle nudging, prompted me. I began shaking, as I felt like every eye was on me. But that night, as I rededicated myself and my son back to Jesus, something extraordinary happened. As the pastor laid his hands on me, a sudden shock surged through my body, leaving me stunned. When I reopened my eyes, I found myself on the floor, covered by a small blanket. Strangely, I was speaking in a tongue I had never spoken before, a mysterious and unfamiliar language that seemed to come from a deep place within me.

The shock that coursed through me as the pastor prayed seemed to signify a profound shift. When I came to, I realized that I had received the Holy Spirit. The unfamiliar tongue I spoke in remained with me, a constant reminder of the divine connection I had forged.

This experience brings to mind the biblical concept of speaking in tongues, as described in

Acts 2:4: "All of them were filled with the Holy Spirit and began to speak in other tongues as the Spirit enabled them."

Just as the disciples spoke in languages they had not known, my newfound tongue served as a powerful reminder of the Holy Spirit's presence and empowerment in my life.

As I immersed myself in my relationship with the Lord, I made another heartfelt declaration. I told Him that unless he Himself brought a man into my life, I was content to live a life dedicated solely to Him. It was an expression of surrender, trust, and a recognition that my ultimate fulfillment would come from my connection with God. As I began going to church, it became a spiritually enlightening experience, but it also triggered moments of self-reflection, lots of repentance, and introspection.

As I reflect on that period of my life, I can vividly recall the early awareness I gained about the possible impact of secular objects within my home on my spiritual journey. Even in my youth, I possessed the ability to experience prophetic dreams, foretelling events that would later unfold. These premonitions often involved the passing of individuals, with their actual departure occurring within weeks of my dreams.

Seeking a deeper understanding of these occurrences, I reached out to various sources, including religious institutions. However, I found that many churches were hesitant to delve into subjects like this, leaving me with unanswered questions. This lack of guidance propelled me towards exploring alternative paths, such as the occult.

Intrigued by the mysteries of the occult, I delved into practices like consulting psychics and utilizing tarot cards. These endeavors provided me with a sense of connection to the supernatural and an avenue to explore the unexplained phenomena I had experienced. This phase of my journey was marked by a quest for answers and a desire to comprehend the intersection between the secular and the spiritual.

Looking back, I recognize how my curiosity and search for meaning led me down the enemy's path, within the exploration of mysticism.

I had a strong desire to begin fostering a more devout environment in my home. With many questions, I went and spoke to the pastor of the church. I shared with him my dreams, I repented about my use of tarot cards, and seeking mediums. I then went on to tell him about how my son, now three, had woken up one morning. He had run into my room, his little hand waving in the air, making plane noises. He stopped dead in his tracks, looked at me, and then shouted, "Boom!" He then said, "Mom, in the water, cracked open like an egg." To my astonishment, when I turned on the news, a plane had crashed into the Hudson River.

The weight of my own experiences had transformed into what felt like an unbreakable curse. The dreams that had once held the allure of foresight had often left me bewildered and perplexed. The inability to grasp their meaning or navigate their intricate messages had left me feeling like a ship lost at sea. Now, as I gazed upon my son, my heart ached with a fierce determination to spare him from this enigmatic burden. I yearned for him to walk a path unburdened by the same cryptic dreams, to be free from the confusion that had clouded my own journey. His future held the promise of a fresh canvas, and I was resolute in my quest to decipher the mysteries that had eluded me, so that he could navigate life's twists and turns with clarity and understanding.

The pastor emphasized that what might appear as a curse was, in fact, a unique prophetic gifting. He elaborated that God often grants individuals special abilities that can be misunderstood by others. Just like how prophets in the Bible faced challenges, this gifting was meant to be a powerful tool for bringing about positive change and enlightenment, rather than a negative force. He encouraged me to see it as a divine calling and to embrace its potential for good.

The church leaders visited my home a day later and together we prayed for Nathaniel, asking the Lord to protect him so that he wouldn't be burdened with dreams until both of us gained a clear understanding of the meaning behind this biblical gift.

I resolved to let go of a lot of my worldly possessions, understanding that by doing so, I could create a space that nurtured my son and me in our spiritual growth, fostering a closer relationship with Jesus. Embracing this change, I embarked on a meaningful journey of purifying my surroundings and aligning them with my newfound spiritual path.

In placing my trust in the Lord's divine plan, I released the need to seek fulfillment solely in human relationships and material things. I embraced the idea that my purpose and joy could be found in serving and loving Jesus, regardless of whether I had worldly treasures or I would ever remarry.

This surrender to God's will allowed me to fully invest in my spiritual journey, deepening my understanding and knowledge. I discovered the beauty of a relationship with Jesus, one that surpasses any earthly connection. He became my comforter, my companion, and the source of my contentment.

During this pivotal time in my life, I wholeheartedly engrossed myself in reading scripture. My dreams, along with Nathaniel's, ceased for a season. With each turn of the sacred pages, I embarked on a profound journey. The scriptures bestowed upon me invaluable insights into the complexities of human nature and how, even when someone failed, if they trusted God, he always made a way out. As I immersed myself in the timeless teachings, I found clarity amidst life's uncertainties and a profound sense of purpose.

The wisdom embedded in each verse offered hope during moments of doubt and strength during my own storms and trials. In my studies, the scriptures began to give me the gift of discernment. I learned to see the interconnectedness of all beings. I began to see others' pain. I began to see others' insecurities. I also saw in context the gifts the Lord bestowed on believers and the enemy's relentless tactics to get us off God's path for our lives.

I began to have the ability to perceive and recognize the true nature of things, situations, or people, especially in a spiritual or moral context. I was aware I had a keen sense of insight, judgment, and intuition, if you will. It enabled me to distinguish between right and wrong, truth and deception, and to make wise decisions based on my perceptions. This gift began allowing me to navigate complex situations with more clarity.

Scripture is more than just ancient texts. It is breath to our lungs; it is the living word that continues to resonate with me and many believers across generations. Its timeless truths and profound teachings transcend time and cultural barriers, breathing life into the hearts of those who seek God.

The power of scripture lies in its ability to speak to me and other individuals in a deeply personal way. As people engage with its sacred pages, they find themselves encountering divine truths and experiencing transformative encounters. The living Word, etched in a book by scribes and guided by the Holy Spirit, remains an unwavering source of spiritual nourishment. We feed our bodies daily. We need to also feed our spirits.

Through this deepening connection with the Lord, the experience of gaining new and profound insights from a familiar book in the Bible with each reading was a testament to the depth and complexity of the scripture. The human mind's ability to connect with the text on various levels, coupled with changing life experiences and perspectives, allowed for a continuously evolving understanding of the material. This dynamic interaction between me and the text showcased the Bible's timeless wisdom and relevance, offering fresh perspectives and lessons that resonated differently based on where I was on my personal journey. It's a beautiful illustration of how spiritual growth and intellectual exploration intersect to deepen one's relationship with our savior.

This surrender to a life of devotion and service became a testament to the transformative power of God's love. It allowed me to release any pressure or expectation to find love in the traditional sense, instead finding fulfillment in the everlasting love of the Lord.

During that particular season, my work schedule consisted of twelve-hour shifts Friday through Sunday while Nathaniel was with his father. I was truly fortunate to have the opportunity to stay at home with my son Monday through Friday, providing him with constant love, care, and support during those crucial early years.

I still remember how excited I was when he read Revelation 22:17, which says, "The Spirit and the bride say, 'Come!' And let him who hears say, 'Come!' Whoever is thirsty, let him come; and whoever wishes, let him take the free gift of the water of life." This verse speaks of the invitation for all to come and partake in the spiritual blessings offered by God. His little toddler voice often echoes in my memory. Let him who hears say, "COME!"

This arrangement not only strengthened my bond with my son but also enabled me to maintain a stable work schedule while being a provider and protector. It proved to be a blessing in so many ways. Night shifts granted me a lot of downtime to engage in a meaningful activity close to my heart—reading the Bible.

The extended breaks during those long night shifts provided the perfect opportunity to immerse myself in the Word and glean more understanding and wisdom from its profound teachings. I found peace and tranquility in the hushed environment of the night, as it truly allowed me to connect more deeply. The silence of the night seemed to amplify the impact of the Bible's words, making each passage resonate even more powerfully within me. The deeper I delved, the more I discovered the profound beauty and relevance of its teachings.

It was a transformative period that not only helped me navigate through the demands of being a single mother, but I also deepened my spiritual journey, leaving a lasting imprint on my life.

Genesis

Superman

Philippians 4:13

I can do all things through him who strengthens me.

I wholeheartedly placed my trust in the Lord, dedicating my love and faith to Him. Despite my devotion, there was still a longing within me. I was only thirty-two years old.

The Lord knew the deepest desires of my heart, and I now know He understood this yearning. With faith as my companion, I embarked on a journey of patience and hope, trusting that in His time, the right companion and father for Nathaniel would be brought into our lives if that was His will.

Drawing inspiration from Gideon's story in Judges 6:36-40, where he tested the Lord's will by using a fleece, I cleverly navigated my search for a life partner. Employing a unique approach, I asked for outrageous confirmations whenever seeking the qualities I sought in a husband. Like Gideon's fleece that absorbed dew, it would help me discern the true essence of the partner I was seeking.

Things like:

"Lord, if it is your desire for me to have a husband, I know you will place him on my doorstep."

"Lord, make him a man of God after your own heart."

"Lord, make him talk and speak of the deeper things."

"Lord, make him an interpreter of dreams for Nathaniel and me."

"Lord, bring me someone who will eat mushrooms out of a can."

"Lord, bring me someone who will have strange quirks like me."

"Lord, make him have all the qualities of a godly husband. Let him have love, patience, kindness, understanding, respect, leadership, and the ability to provide and protect."

"Lord, let him have communication skills, faithfulness, and a willingness to serve and support me and Nathaniel."

Listen you guys, I can honestly see the Lord chuckling at me as one night I even wrote my request in a journal.

I know His love was truly enough, and my trust in Him would lead me on a path of abundant blessings and divine guidance.

Three years after my divorce, a remarkable turn of events unfolded. On social media, I had the unexpected opportunity to reconnect with someone from my past. He was merely an acquaintance I had known during my school days.

As we spoke more frequently, he shared his experiences and the challenges of his addiction and recovery. It was fascinating how I began to realize how small the world can sometimes feel. I discovered that his brother and my brother were incredibly close throughout their school years, sharing a bond that I had no idea about. Additionally, I learned that my parents stood up for his aunt and uncle at their wedding.

These revelations served as a reminder of the unexpected connections and shared experiences that tie us all together in this vast world. Our encounters on social media led to profound conversations about Jesus. His vulnerability and transparency continued to enlighten me about the grace given to us, as I myself had never experienced drug addiction.

I enjoyed our conversations and then there was a tragic event. I received the news that my grandmother had suffered a heart attack. It was a devastating moment. I immediately traveled to Mississippi to be by her side and support my family during this difficult time. However, upon our arrival, I learned that her condition was critical, and she wouldn't have a chance for survival or any quality of life.

It was heart-wrenching to make the decision to leave my son in the care of his father, but I knew it was essential to be with my grandmother and to be able to say my final goodbyes. Supporting my mother through this emotional journey was also crucial, as we leaned on each other for strength during those trying days.

On the third day, I had to embark on the journey home. I couldn't help but feel a strange mix of emotions—traveling alone, rushing through terminals to catch new flights. But most of all, I was returning home while my grandmother was transitioning to be with Jesus. This was incredibly tough for me. I felt a whirlwind of emotions swirling within me.

On one hand, there was a deep sadness knowing I couldn't be by her side during such a significant moment. On the other hand, there was a conflicting sense of responsibility for needing to return home. My commitments were truly in caring for my son, and I couldn't overlook that responsibility. It's like my heart was torn between wanting to be with my grandmother and ensuring my son's well-being. I struggled with feelings of guilt, wondering if I should have made different choices.

The distance added to the emoti'nal strain. Not being there physically meant missing out on the opportunity to hold her hand and be present in her final moments. It's hard to shake off the regret of not being able to create those last memories together.

Despite these challenging emotions, I found peace in the belief that she was going to be with our Savior. While I wasn't there to witness her transition, I held on to the hope that she's in a better place, free from pain and suffering. Death is always a complex journey of grief and acceptance.

I had many losses during childhood—my maternal grandfather, paternal grandparents, and my best friend's mother. I don't think you truly grasp loss at a young age. Grief in losing a loved one can be particularly challenging due to the depth of the emotional bond that has been established over time. The longer the relationship, the more intertwined the lives and memories become, intensifying the pain of the loss. This emotional investment makes the grieving process harder, as it involves not just mourning the person, but also the shared experiences, dreams, and future plans.

The passage of time often means that the person who is lost has become an integral part of one's daily routine and support system. Their absence can create a void that is difficult to fill.

As people age, we undoubtedly accumulate more losses, and the cumulative effect of multiple losses can magnify the intensity of grief. When losing a loved one in adulthood, we also grapple with our own mortality and the realization that the number of years we have left to share with others is finite.

All these factors combined, I believe, make grief at losing a loved one so much harder in adulthood.

As an adult, I learned to navigate. It was through my grandmother that I found guidance and learned all about heaven.

Through our conversations and scripture reading, I learned heaven is a place of eternal joy, peace, and perfection promised to believers. It is described as a dwelling place with God, where there is no pain, sorrow, or suffering. One of the most well-known descriptions of heaven is found in Revelation 21:1-5. "Then I saw 'a new heaven and a new earth,' for the first heaven and the first earth had passed away, and there was no longer any sea. I saw the Holy City, the new Jerusalem, coming down out of heaven from God, prepared as a bride beautifully dressed for her husband. And I heard a loud voice from the throne saying, 'Look! God's dwelling place is now among the people, and he will dwell with them. They will be his people, and God himself will be with them and be their God. He will wipe every tear from their eyes. There will be no more death or mourning or crying or pain, for the old order of things has passed away.'"

This passage paints a vivid picture of the glorious heaven, where God's presence brings ultimate healing and restoration. In this heavenly realm, all the brokenness and pain experienced on Earth will be washed away, and believers will be fully healed in body, mind, and spirit.

Although we may face challenges and never experience complete healing on Earth, we can find hope in the promise of heaven.

Philippians 3:20-21 reminds us of our citizenship in heaven: "But our citizenship is in heaven. And we eagerly await a Savior from there, the Lord Jesus Christ, who, by the power that enables him to bring everything under his control, will transform our lowly bodies so that they will be like his glorious body."

Through faith in Jesus Christ, we have the assurance that one day we will be completely transformed, free from all the limitations and brokenness of this world. In heaven, we will experience the fullness of God's love and be in perfect communion with Him, leading to true and everlasting healing for our souls.

My grandmother played a profound role in introducing me to the teachings of Jesus. Through her words, actions, and unwavering faith, she showed me the path of love, compassion, and selflessness that Jesus exemplified. Her life was a living testament to these principles, and her guidance made it easy for me to eventually find solace in my mourning.

The foundation of faith she helped me build enabled me to see her passing not just as a loss, but as a continuation of her journey in the presence of Jesus. As I mourned her departure, her example of living a life aligned with Christ's teachings made the process of saying goodbye a little easier, knowing that she had found her eternal home with the Savior she loved and followed.

On my journey home, in an unexpected moment, the pilot announced over the intercom that we were flying over Spartanburg, South Carolina, where Kenny lived. It felt like a God wink—a meaningful coincidence— as Kenny was someone who held special significance in my life, and this connection brought a sense of comfort during a difficult time.

What is a God wink you may ask? My life is full of them.

A "God wink" is a concept that suggests the existence of spiritual connections in our lives. I describe it as instances of serendipity, meaningful coincidences, or events that seem to be too perfect or timely to be mere chance. People who believe in God winks interpret these occurrences as signs or messages from our divine creator or even spiritual discernment or intuition.

God winks are not all necessarily associated with any specific religious belief; rather, they speak to the idea that there is a greater force or energy at play in the universe that guides us and communicates with us through these meaningful occurrences. Some people may see them as reassurances, reminders, or answers to prayers.

For example, a person might be contemplating an important decision and, suddenly, a song with just the right lyrics plays on the radio, seemingly addressing their concerns. Or someone might be going through a difficult time, and a long-lost friend unexpectedly reaches out with the exact support they needed. In many cases in my travels for work I may be praying for answers, and I will see a license plate that has significant dates or abbreviations like KING 1777, or a semi-truck with the logo such as swift or covenant transport.

My interpretation of a God wink is that it can be highly personal and subjective, varying based on an individual's beliefs and experiences. Some may find great comfort and inspiration in these occurrences as I do, while others may see them as mere coincidences.

Nevertheless, the concept of God winks remain a fascinating aspect of my personal life and how I perceive and find meaning in some of the events of my life.

Just like in the midst of my grief and heartache, these little signs can provide moments of enlightenment, reminding us that there is a larger assembling of connections and meaning in our lives. Despite the sadness.

And then a suddenly happened.

"Suddenly" is an adverb that indicates an unexpected or abrupt occurrence of an action or event. When something happens suddenly, it happens very quickly and without warning, catching people by surprise. It implies that there is little or no anticipation or preparation for the event or action that took place. For example, if someone suddenly appeared at your doorstep, it means they arrived unexpectedly and without prior notice.

That Christmas Eve, that's exactly what happened, seven months after my grandmother's passing. A "suddenly" happened. Kenny had traveled six hundred miles to visit family and arrived unexpectedly and "suddenly" at my doorstep.

As I opened the door to see him standing there, I felt a surge of emotions—surprise, curiosity, and a sense of divine intervention. It was a moment filled with the recognition that this reunion was not a mere coincidence, but a providential alignment and confirmation orchestrated by the hand of God.

His presence was undeniable, and he exuded a sense of unwavering determination that reminded me of the legendary Superman. From the moment I first saw him, it was as if a powerful aura surrounded him, much like the iconic superhero who stood for truth, justice, and the greater good.

But it wasn't just his character that resonated with the Man of Steel; it was his physical appearance, too. His hair, in particular, caught my attention with its confident little flip to the side. It seemed to mirror Superman's trademark curl, as if fate had designed it to be a subtle nod to the comic book hero.

As he walked into my living room, his magnetic charisma made it impossible not to be captivated by his presence. He displayed a genuine warmth and concern that mirrored Superman's caring nature. As he took off his coat, I noticed his arms were tattooed with magnificent colors. As I caught sight of his arms and their tattoos for the first time, the vibrant colors immediately drew my attention. Each stroke of ink seemed to tell a story, and as we began to discuss them, I learned that these tattoos symbolized more than just artwork. He shared how each design represented a trial he had faced and overcome, much like the journey of Superman. The vibrant hues mirrored the resilience that he had displayed in the face of challenges, transforming his scars into badges of strength. I began to understand not only the physical beauty of his tattoos but also the emotional depth and triumph they embodied.

Like the superhero who selflessly saves lives, during this time he seemed ready to lend a helping hand. He assisted me in wrapping Nathaniel's

Christmas gifts and his strong sense of empathy was evident in the way he listened and supported me. He carried himself with quiet confidence.

As I got to know him better, I couldn't help but draw more parallels between him and the Man of Steel. Just like Superman's alter ego, Clark Kent, he was down-to-earth and approachable.

Of course, he was just a regular person like anyone else. He may not have had superpowers or wore a cape, but he possessed qualities that were equally heroic.

As we enjoyed each other's company over the next few days, we found enlightenment and understanding in our shared journeys. Together, we reflected on the transformative power of Jesus and how it had brought healing and purpose into both of our lives.

In this unexpected reunion, we discovered that our paths had converged once again, not only as friends but also as companions on the journey of faith. Our connection was a testament to the continued will of God, who had brought us both from two different places, to a path knitted together in mysterious and extraordinary ways.

We reminisced about our adolescence and the rebellion we both had walked in. We never hung around in the same crowds. We found humor in the idea that without that unseen guidance, Jesus, we might have ended up working for the wrong kingdom. It's almost like a cosmic joke that we narrowly avoided meeting each other. Our shared laughter underscored the gratitude we felt that God's timing is always perfect.

The Lord's gu'dance often manifests through unique confirmations, speaking to individuals in deeply personal and profound manners. I found assurance through unexpected signs, signs I had asked for, like eating mushrooms straight out of a can which I watched him do as I made dinner one evening. While studying scriptures with him, I quickly discovered explanation points with hearts where the period should be. They were scattered throughout his Bible. This was a unique and distinct way I had always made mine when I wrote and something I had done since middle school. I still don't think he would have believed me until I showed him my journals. These seemingly ordinary occurrences to him, took on a huge spiritual significance to me, serving as confirmations from God.

I gleaned much understanding from his interpretation of my dream journal. He had so much wisdom and knowledge and truly was a man after God's heart. Each interpretation was backed by the scripture he shared. Such moments of divine connection were awe-inspiring to me, reaffirming the belief in a God that communicates through the most intricate and intimate details of our lives.

During that special Christmas season, our bond deepened as we celebrated the birth of Christ and the incredible gift of redemption. We recognized that our meeting on Christmas Eve was a tangible reminder of the compassion that Jesus extends to all, regardless of our past mistakes or struggles.

Together, we embarked on a new journey. Our shared experiences and understanding of the power of God created a strong foundation for our friendship, rooted in mutual support, vulnerability, and a shared commitment to following Jesus.

As the months unfolded, our relationship continued to evolve. We became constants in each other's life. We would seek the word of God through calls and emails, comparing notes and digging into deeper meanings through the use of a strong concordance, something he showed me. Through our friendship, studying the word, we found strength and inspiration.

Looking back, I see the hand of God working in remarkable ways orchestrating our reconnection, bringing us together on that meaningful Christmas Eve. It was a powerful reminder that God's timing is perfect and that His plans often unfold in ways we cannot fully comprehend.

In the person who arrived on my doorstep that Christmas Eve, I found a kindred spirit—a fellow traveler who understood my depth. The Bible says the deep calls out to deep. Our reconnection became a testament to the unfathomable ways in which God weaves the stories of our lives together.

And through it all, I give thanks for that fateful Christmas Eve when God's mercy and love showed up on my doorstep, forever changing the trajectory of my life.

Kryptonite

Proverbs 28:13

He who conceals his transgressions will not prosper, but he who confesses and forsakes them will find compassion.

Kenny made another visit in April. Unbeknownst to me, he made a visit to my parents and asked for the blessing of my hand in marriage. He arrived at my home and as we set out for dinner, he said he had something in the glove box for me. As I rummaged through, there was a tiny box and within it was a beautiful gold ring with a heart in the middle and three diamonds set within.

He asked me to marry him and shared the meaning behind the ring. It was an heirloom of his mother's. More importantly it signified the Father, The Son and the Holy spirit that would represent and guide us in our upcoming life together.

A new chapter of my life began and when June arrived, Kenny moved from South Carolina, his books and car the only thing in tow. We exchanged our vows on July 7th, 2011. The significance of the date, with its repetition of the number seven, held deep meaning for us both. In the Bible, the number seven symbolizes completion, a fitting representation of the journey we were embarking upon.

Our union was not without its challenges and complexities. Kenny, who was a welder, secured a fabricator job a few months after our marriage. Unfortunately, he faced intense persecution from fellow employees due to his practice of sharing his faith and witnessing to others about Jesus. I believe the Lord was truly showing him the aspects of evangelizing, but this led to multiple warnings from the company owner. Kenny remained steadfast in his beliefs. Despite his efforts, the situation escalated and ultimately resulted in his dismissal. The company extended a settlement offer as a resolution. I admired Kenny's courage in standing up for his convictions, even in the face of adversity.

Our journey was marked by many new experiences and trials. A year later I was met with headaches that persisted for over a week and the realization of a missed period sunk in. I felt a sense of curiosity and concern. Wanting to put my suspicions to rest, Kenny hurried to the store and picked up a pregnancy test. The minutes that followed were filled with anticipation and anxiety as we waited for the results. To our surprise and joy, the test displayed a positive sign, confirming the presence of new life.

The mixture of emotions, from excitement to a touch of nervousness, marked the beginning of a journey I hadn't anticipated but was now embracing with open arms. Kenny had never had biological children of his own and I was in awe of the goodness of God due to my history with fertility issues.

Three months into my pregnancy, my best friend Jenn was by my side during my first ultrasound. Kenny was unable to attend due to his work schedule. It was an experience I'll always treasure. As we gazed at the monitor, we marveled at the sight of tiny, delicate hands and feet. It was an incredible moment that brought tears to my eyes.

But what really caught my attention was the boundless energy of this little one. The ultrasound technician had a bit of a challenge keeping up with all the movement. It felt like this baby was dancing in my now round stomach.

Comparing this experience to when I was pregnant with Nathaniel, who hardly moved, it was clear that each baby had their own unique personality from the very beginning. Nathaniel's stillness contrasted with the vibrant energy of this new baby, and it filled me with excitement and wonder about the journey ahead.

A week later as I was in the kitchen of our new home washing dishes, I felt some cramping in my lower abdomen. Then a gush of what I thought was water coursed down my pant leg.

On further inspection I realized I had begun to bleed. I called my doctor. He assured me that bleeding was sometimes nothing to be alarmed by. As the evening went on, it only persisted with greater intensity. I relented as I called Kenny home from work. We then made our way to the hospital. After speaking with doctors and nurses they prepared me for an ultrasound. Undergoing an ultrasound can be an anxious but hopeful experience for expecting parents. But the atmosphere was thick. The ultrasound technician glided the wand over my now growing belly. I listened intently, seeking the reassuring sound of the baby's heartbeat. However, as the minutes stretched on, a growing sense of unease settled in the room. The technician's brow furrowed, her movements becoming more deliberate as she searched for the elusive rhythm that should have echoed through the monitor. The silence hung heavy, a stark contrast to the eager heartbeats of Kenny and I. Time seemed to stand still as the technician's efforts yielded no results, leaving everyone caught in a surreal moment of uncertainty, hoping for a positive turn of events. She could not find a heartbeat and we were informed that I was likely miscarrying.

They sent us home and told us to follow up with my doctor the following day. We spent the evening crying and praying that a miracle would happen, that the gift God had given us would not be taken away.

Arriving at the doctor's office with a mixture of anticipation and apprehension, we held onto a glimmer of hope that this visit would bring about a profound shift in our circumstances. After undergoing yet another ultrasound, the atmosphere again grew heavy with tension as reality began to sink in: the news remained unchanged. With heavy hearts, we listened as the doctor gently informed us that I was experiencing a miscarriage. The weight of the moment was overwhelming, and emotions swirled as we navigated the somber reality before us. As the doctor's words settled in, I couldn't help but notice the tears that welled up in my husband's eyes as he laid his head on my stomach. It was an unfamiliar sight, the first time I had witnessed him succumb to such raw vulnerability. His tears, akin to the mythical kryptonite weakening Superman, revealed the depth of our shared pain and shattered expectations. In that moment, our strength wavered, and we clung to each other for support amidst the emotional storm that had suddenly enveloped us.

Three days later I would be admitted to the hospital where they would remove my lifeless baby from my womb. We entered into a period of grief together, both desperately wanting healing in a tragedy that would leave us grappling with our faith and questioning the very fabric of our lives.

Through the devastating loss of my precious baby, I found myself grappling with profound questions about God and the unpredictability of life. The pain and sorrow I experienced was overwhelming, leading me to question why this could happen. In my grief, I longed for a reality where my baby would still be with me, cherishing the moments that would never come to pass. The journey of healing was challenging, but it has also provided space for reflection and a deeper understanding of the complexities of existence.

While years later the ache remains, I came to a realization that if I could not rock my baby in my arms, what better place to be than in the arms of Jesus for eternity.

During my time in the hospital, my mother and mother-in-law were there to support Kenny and I. I remember Kenny's mother leaving abruptly after my procedure. Kenny's stepsister was pregnant as well. She had gone into labor hours before our arrival at the hospital. Experiencing the loss of my baby was an incredibly difficult and painful moment. The emotions of grief and heartache were overwhelming, making it hard to process the reality of the situation. Struggling with this immense loss, I found myself grappling with a contrasting juxtaposition. On the same day that I faced my own sorrow, the world celebrated the birth of another precious life. The simultaneous occurrence of these two deeply contrasting events served as a stark reminder of life's unpredictable nature, its highs and lows intertwined in a complex web of emotions.

A week later, as we gathered for a family function, his sister extended an invitation to hold her newborn daughter. Initially hesitant, I eventually accepted, with Kenny by my side. She asked everyone to give us private time. As we cradled the delicate bundle, tears streamed down our faces, carrying with them a profound sense of healing. The cycle of life and the innocence of the new life before us provided peace, reminding us that even in the face of pain and hardship, there is still room for hope and renewal.

As the weeks continued on, the pain proved to be overwhelming for Kenny, and he struggled to cope with the grief. Despite our efforts, the emotional burden was immense, making it challenging for him.

One evening, I returned home after spending the afternoon at a local lake with my son. I put Nathaniel to bed. Moments Later Kenny emerged and came in from the living room where I had assumed he had been sleeping. I won't go into all the grave details of that night, only the pertinent ones.

I began to feel overwhelmed and concerned with his slurred speech and unrecognizable mannerisms.

I see the hand of God in every aspect of that night as this would become my first lesson on spiritual warfare.

Kenny's behavior became increasingly erratic, causing unease to gnaw at the edges of my mind. I silently prayed for his deliverance from whatever demons had taken hold of him. It became very obvious he was under the influence of some unknown substance or force that I was not privy to. His behavior transformed into one of mockery and disdain. He seemed compelled to taunt me, his words laced with a cruel edge. Something I had never heard or seen in my husband.

The situation began to feel as if it was spiraling out of control, and the unsettling events unfolding before me left me with a chilling sense of foreboding. With each passing moment, the atmosphere grew more charged, the energy practically crackling in the air. My instinct for self-preservation kicked in, urging me to distance myself from the escalating chaos. I ran to Nathaniel's room and quietly shook him awake, my growing concern overpowering any hesitation. As I began to silently pray, I became louder and louder, and an unexpected shift occurred. I gained my composure, and a peace fell over me. Kenny began to yell from upstairs, "Where are you? Are you hiding from me?"

I quietly nudged Nathaniel to walk in front of me to the foyer, putting my finger over my lips to hush him. As I turned to walk out the door, an unexpected twist occurred. Kenny was standing there behind me. Driven by some inexplicable impulse, he lunged towards me grabbing my purse and hurling it up the stairs with a reckless abandon. To my disbelief, as the bag collided with the steps, the unmistakable jingle of my keys reached my ears. The keys had fallen, landing right onto my foot in an eerie and twisted indication that it was time to depart from this disconcerting scene.

I continued to pray, my son now standing in the driveway by my car. Me, trapped in the doorway. I began pleading for my husband's deliverance, when Kenny abruptly turned and walked away, leaving behind a sense of unease. The moment held an eerie and inexplicable quality, as if my actions had triggered his departure, raising questions about the source of his behavior and the power of the prayer.

In that surreal moment, a strange feeling of divine intervention washed over me. It was as though God was steering me away from the danger that had manifested within those walls. With a heavy heart and a mix of fear and relief, I grabbed my keys that had landed on my foot and ran out of the house, exchanging a quick glance with Nathaniel, so he knew to get in the car quickly.

As we stepped into the safety of my vehicle, the incident served as a stark reminder that there are moments when we must heed the signs presented to us, even if they come in the most unexpected and unsettling forms. I drove quickly to my parents' house. Upon arriving I called the police and told them of the occurrence that had happened so that they could check on Kenny's well-being.

The officers arrived promptly and recognized the seriousness of the situation. They arrested Kenny for his behavior and took him into custody.

In the following days, Kenny faced multiple court appearances due to his actions. I too had to face the judge as a temporary protection order was put into place by the state of Ohio. Although I did not want to file any charges, I had to talk to and be questioned multiple times by prosecutors, attorneys, and judges. In the face of their assumptions that Kenny had been abusive toward me, I stood firm and unwavering in my conviction. I spoke my truth with resolute honesty, recounting the incident, resolute that in the span of two years, this had been the first and only instance where I had witnessed him behaving in this manner. I refused to let assumptions overshadow the reality I had experienced. Through my unwavering testimony, I aimed to bring clarity to the situation and ensure that my voice was heard, enabling a fair and balanced understanding of the circumstances at hand. It was a challenging time for me, Nathaniel, and our family, as we had to cope with the repercussions of Kenny's actions.

Amidst turmoil, I found solace in my faith, witnessing God's hand in every moment. Kenny's failure to find me in Nathaniel's room, my keys landing perfectly, and his sudden departure all seemed divinely orchestrated. Through prayer, I sought strength and guidance, yearning to uncover the next best step for Nathaniel and myself. One night, as I was deep in prayer in my childhood room, I felt a strong sense of faith and heard a voice within my heart, guiding me to stand for my marriage and consider forgiveness.

I opened my bible, and it landed on Psalm 32:8: "I will instruct you and teach you in the way you should go; I will counsel you with my loving eye on you."

I struggled with this message, torn between my love for Kenny and the need to protect myself and son. I sought counsel from my close friends, pastors, my parents, and even spoke with a counselor to help me navigate through these difficult emotions.

As weeks turned into months, I saw changes in Kenny. He was living at the local court-ordered Oriana house. He started attending support groups, acknowledging his drug addiction, and seeking professional help. The journey to recovery was long and challenging, but I held onto hope and faith, and so did Kenny.

Throughout this process, I found the strength to forgive Kenny for his past actions, but I remained cautious and vigilant. I insisted on open communication to heal our relationship and rebuild trust.

Kenny showed genuine remorse and repentance for his behavior, and his commitment to change shone through. We began to rebuild our family with love, understanding, and a newfound appreciation for each other.

Our journey was far from easy, but it taught us valuable lessons about the power of forgiveness, second chances, and the importance of seeking help when needed. He spent six long months away from my son and I, seeking treatment and fighting his inner demons. The pain of separation weighed heavily on both of us.

Kenny was still godly in many ways; he was a remarkable provider, displaying unwavering dedication throughout his journey of recovery. Despite the challenges he faced, his determination to continue to provide for his family was evident in the way he forged through. He never lost sight of his responsibilities and the love he held for us.

Two years had passed since Kenny's last relapse, and it pained me deeply to see him experiencing yet another setback. The relentless grip of addiction had tightened its hold yet again, and he began using opiates leaving both of us questioning the reasons behind this distressing recurrence.

I found myself wrestling with a sense of helplessness as I struggled to comprehend why he made the choices he did. Was it the lack of continuing support groups that contributed to this relapse? Was it the constant physical pain from injuries that had him seeking multiple doctors for opiates, or were there other hidden triggers and complexities that remained hidden from my view?

Kenny's journey was marked by a painful beginning, as he had experienced childhood trauma that would shape his path ahead. The earliest remembrance he shared was at the age of three. These early wounds left deep scars, influencing his emotions and behaviors as he grew older. At the tender age of thirteen, Kenny found himself facing a pivotal moment when he entered his first treatment center to address his burgeoning addiction.

The trauma from his past had created a void within Kenny, leading him to seek substances that temporarily numbed his pain. The weight of his experiences had become too much to bear, and he turned to alcohol and drugs as a means of escape. His young age made him particularly vulnerable, and the lack of healthy coping mechanisms only exacerbated his struggles.

The inner demons of addiction are elusive and insidious, shrouded in a labyrinth of emotions, memories, and traumas he held on his own and still seem impossible to fully grasp.

Addiction doesn't discriminate based on factors like race, social standing, or ethnicity. It can affect anyone, regardless of their background. Addiction can impact people from all walks of life, highlighting that it's a complex issue rooted in physiological, psychological, and environmental factors rather than societal distinctions. This began to teach me the importance of understanding addiction as a health concern or disease that required support, treatment, and compassion for all individuals affected, regardless of their personal attributes.

As I stood by Kenny's side, my heart ached for him, wishing I could offer definitive answers and solutions to ease his pain. I know how vital supportive networks and resources are for those on the path to recovery, but sometimes the allure of addiction can be overwhelming, even in the presence of such support. I reminded myself that I could never fully understand the intricacies of what he was going through, for it is a deeply personal battle, and was shaped by his unique experiences and struggles.

When explaining drug addiction to others, I always like to remind people we all struggle with some type of addiction. I believe drawing a comparison between drug addiction and an addiction to cheeseburgers can reveal interesting insights into the nature of addiction. Just like a cheeseburger, drugs are very accessible. Of course, they are starkly different in terms of their impact and consequences. While a cheeseburger addiction can lead to health issues, drug addiction carries far more serious physical, mental, spiritual, and social repercussions. The seemingly easy availability of both can be deceiving, as the allure of instant gratification masks the long-term harm that can result. It's important to recognize the complexities of addiction and its potential to profoundly affect individuals' lives.

Over the years I have come to the belief that sin is sin, whether it involves a cheeseburger, pornography, homosexuality, drug addiction, or alcohol abuse. In my view, all of these actions stem from an attempt to fill a void or mask emotional pain. I see these behaviors as responses to inner struggles, reflecting the idea that they are not just isolated actions, but manifestations of deeper emotional or psychological challenges. This belief just underscores my understanding that many human actions are driven by underlying motivations and needs.

Despite the uncertainties, I had to make yet another decision. So I prayed and ultimately left and moved in with my best friend and her husband. In the depths of my unwavering commitment to Kenny, I became consumed by the fervor of our relationship. Although I had left, I began prioritizing him and my son above all else.

It was a love that felt all-encompassing, and I believed that nothing could shake the foundation we had built. Little did I know that this single-minded dedication would come at a heavy cost.

As I devoted more time and energy to trying to get Kenny the help he needed, I inadvertently started neglecting the bonds that had once held my life together. My family, who had always been my support, felt increasingly distant as I focused on God, my partner, and son.

Friends who had stood by me through thick and thin began to drift away. I began to feel neglected and unimportant.

Even within my professional life, my dedication to Kenny started taking a toll. I found myself less focused at work, distracted by thoughts of him and our relationship. My performance began to suffer, leading to missed time and missed opportunities that ultimately resulted in my hours being cut.

The first understanding of codependency hit me like a tidal wave. It was a combination of feelings as I also felt abandoned by the people I once held dear and facing the harsh reality of the loss of finances due to my own choices. The pain of it all cut deep, I also felt like drugs had become a mistress and I felt an overwhelming sense of loneliness and regret.

In the midst of this turmoil, I started reflecting on the path I had taken and the consequences of my actions. I realized that my unwavering commitment to Kenny had led me astray, and in the process, I had lost touch with the aspects of my life that were equally vital for my well-being.

We did share an inexplicable connection that dictated the flow of my days. There were days and nights I would have this fleeting flutter in my chest. Although separated, we still spoke daily on the phone. I learned quickly when this happened more often than not, he was using drugs. It gave becoming one flesh a whole new understanding.

When Kenny experienced a bad day, it was as if my own world mirrored his struggles, resulting in me having a challenging day as well. Conversely, on days when Kenny's spirits were high, and he was brimming with positivity, my day would unfold in a remarkably bright and cheerful manner.

So when Kenny had a good day, Jody had a good day, and when Kenny had a bad day, Jody had a bad day.

Our intertwined emotional states had reached a point where my moods seemed to dictate his experiences. This phenomenon, although puzzling to outsiders, had become a defining characteristic of our relationship. It was as though I had become codependent to his emotions, with my feelings intertwined in a complex dance that neither of us fully understood.

On the surface, this symbiotic connection might have seemed heartwarming, indicative of our deep bond. However, as time went on, it became clear that this codependency was not necessarily healthy. My emotional well-being hinged on his daily experiences, leaving me vulnerable to the ebb and flow of life's ups and downs.

While supporting him through tough times was an essential aspect of our relationship, relying solely on someone else's emotional state for our own well-being had led to an unhealthy imbalance. It was important for me to develop a sense of emotional autonomy and resilience, even when we shared such a close connection.

I eventually recognized the need to address this codependent pattern. This was when I began reading about codependency. Codependency refers to a psychological and behavioral pattern where one person in a relationship (me) excessively relies on and feels responsible for meeting the emotional and physical needs of another person, often at the expense of their own well-being. It typically involves a lack of healthy boundaries, an overemphasis on pleasing others, and a sense of control or validation through the relationship. Codependency can be found in various types of relationships, such as romantic partnerships, family dynamics, and friendships. It often leads to unhealthy dynamics, enabling behaviors, and difficulties in maintaining a balanced sense of self.

It was a turning point that made me appreciate the significance of balance and the importance of nurturing all the relationships in my life, not just one. I began the journey of rebuilding those connections years later when the Lord gave me more insight and the hopes of restoration and reconciliation.

But through this difficult period, I learned that codependency, though painful, can be a catalyst for growth and self-discovery. It taught me the value of resilience and adaptability, and the necessity of recognizing the needs of both myself and those I care about.

Leaving was difficult, but I couldn't shake the thought of my vows that included "in sickness and in health." I had formed my own perspective that addiction should be seen as a disease. During that period, I held the belief that the only biblically justifiable reason for divorce was adultery.

In time, I found a sense of harmony in my life, a delicate balance between love and commitment to Kenny and the precious connections that make life fulfilling.

In my continued commitment to stand by Kenny, I forgave him, offering a listening ear, and a compassionate heart while remaining separated. I began to realize that recovery was a journey filled with agonizing setbacks, but I was determined to be there for him every step of the way, but from a distance. I would navigate the maze of addiction's challenges, seeking out resources, counseling, and any other necessary tools to help him overcome these inner demons, while focusing on tools that would also not enable his bad behavior and choices.

In the face of such complexity, I sought biblical guidance, explanations, and as his helpmate I continued to urge him to seek professional help, often reminding him of God's grace. Through this ongoing battle, I remained hopeful that one day, Kenny would find the strength and resilience to break free from addiction's clutches.

After a month of using even heavier drugs, the emotional support and protection also had vanished, and a significant portion of our material possessions were sold as his addiction intensified. To make matters worse, my husband also lost his job.

Losing not only the stability of a partner but also the comfort of familiar belongings was a blow that was hard to absorb. The decision to sell off items that held memories and significance to me to buy drugs only deepened my sense of loss. The weight of these changes was overwhelming, and at times, it was as if there was no solid ground to stand on.

In times like these, leaning on the support of friends became my lifeline. Their understanding and encouragement reminded me that my value wasn't tied to material possessions or what seemed like a failed marriage. It was a journey of self-discovery and resilience, as I worked to rebuild my life from the ground up.

Drug addiction is a complex issue that often leads to a skewed focus on the individual struggling with addiction, leaving the immediate family members in the background. Addiction has wide-reaching consequences, affecting not just the addict but also their loved ones. While the intention to help the addict is important, it's equally crucial to recognize the toll it takes on the family's emotional, financial, and psychological well-being.

When people concentrate solely on helping the addict, they might inadvertently neglect the family's needs. I often experienced feelings of guilt, shame, confusion, and anger.

The constant worry about Kenny's well-being and the unpredictable nature of his addiction led to stress and mental health challenges for me and my son.

Also, the financial strain left me struggling to maintain stability. The disruption of our daily routines and my need to constantly address crises truly impacted so many of my relationships and the overall quality of life for everyone involved.

Over the years I've learned offering support and resources to families dealing with addiction is also essential. Providing access to counseling, therapy, support groups, and education can help family members develop coping strategies and find peace in knowing they are not alone in their experiences.

Though the road was tough, the experience taught me that I have an inner strength, "Jesus," that helps me weather even the toughest storms. With time, I started to focus on what truly matters to God and my own well-being. How can you take care of others if you're not taking care of yourself? The challenges I faced during the separation reshaped my perspective and allowed me to embrace change in a way I never thought possible.

I found myself on my knees, crying, begging God for answers. The weight of possibly ending my marriage and losing everything was overwhelming. Through tearful prayers and heartfelt pleas, I sought a sign, a whisper, an answer, anything that could guide me through this painful decision.

Would I endure another divorce? How was this shaping Nathaniel? Where would I live? How would I pay bills? Days turned into weeks, and yet, there was only silence. No divine message, no unmistakable sign, no God wink. I questioned whether I was doing something wrong, whether my pleas were falling on deaf ears. Were my prayers hitting the ceiling? How could a decision of such magnitude be met with such apparent indifference?

But as time passed, I began to see things differently. Maybe the absence of a direct answer was, in itself, an answer. Perhaps I was meant to find the strength within myself to make this choice, to trust my discernment and my own beliefs.

It's not easy to accept that the answers we seek might not arrive in the way we expect. Sometimes, the journey of grappling with our doubts and fears is where we discover our own strength and inner wisdom. While I didn't receive a clear sign from above, I came to understand that the act of reaching out to God and having faith had given me a space to reflect and to find the courage to face my future, whatever it would hold.

Two months into my separation on a weekend Nathaniel was with his father, I pleaded with Ed and Jenn to allow Kenny to come over and speak with me. They hesitantly agreed. I messaged him letting him know that my friends had agreed to allow him to come and speak with me. I also mentioned the time, and I didn't text him again after that. Waiting for him to arrive became challenging. His addiction seemed to be spiraling out of control, and my faith in his ability to show up was dwindling. However, amidst my doubts, a realization struck me: his willingness to show up or not would ultimately provide the answer I was seeking.

The moment he arrived, a sense of urgency and a glimpse of hope filled the air. As we spoke, I felt compelled to reassure him that my love for him remained but that something would have to change. In those moments, I encouraged him to imagine my love for him and then the vast and unconditional love that God had for him being even greater. The memory of that night is still vivid in my mind—his tears streaming down his face as he rested his head on my lap, the same vulnerability he showed when we lost our baby. He gripped my leg like a frightened child, pouring out his pain, his sadness, his frustration releasing his intense emotions.

In that profound exchange, it became evident that something transformative was happening within him. It was as if a divine revelation had touched his heart and soul. The weight of his past mistakes and struggles seemed to find a path outward.

He confided in me in great detail about his childhood, his trauma, how when he grew strength to confide in adults he was accused of lying. My heart broke. But with courage in his eyes, he made the difficult decision to seek yet treatment again.

As I recall those moments, I gain an understanding that drugs possess a haunting similarity to Superman's infamous kryptonite, wielding a formidable power that can weaken and debilitate those who fall prey to their allure. Just as kryptonite strips Superman of his strength and abilities, drugs have the potential to strip away an individual's physical health, mental clarity, spiritual vitality, and emotional stability. The allure of drugs can be captivating, initially offering an escape from life's challenges or a fleeting sense of euphoria.

However, as with kryptonite's adverse effects on the Man of Steel, the use and abuse of drugs can lead to a downward spiral of detrimental consequences.

Much like Superman's vulnerability to kryptonite, individuals who find themselves ensnared in drug addiction become increasingly susceptible to its control, often losing their sense of self and connection to loved ones. The allure of drugs can grow into a relentless grip, fueling a dependency that saps one's willpower and leaves them feeling trapped and powerless. Just as kryptonite's presence lingers, lurking in the shadows, the influence of drugs can permeate every aspect of a person's life, tainting relationships, career aspirations, and overall well-being.

Similarly Superman's fight against kryptonite requires unyielding determination and resilience. Overcoming drug addiction demands an unwavering commitment to recovery. It often involves confronting deep-seated issues, seeking professional help, and building a support network to bolster one's journey toward healing. Just as Superman strives to protect the world from the devastation of kryptonite, society must work together to combat the widespread impact of drug abuse by promoting awareness, education, and access to treatment resources.

In essence, the analogy between drugs and Superman's kryptonite serves as a stark reminder of the destructive power that substances can hold over individuals. It highlights the urgent need for compassionate understanding and effective intervention to break the chains of addiction and help individuals reclaim their lives when they come to the realization that they want and need help. They must seek their sobriety, like they did in active addiction. With the right support and determination, individuals battling drug addiction can find their own inner strength, transforming themselves with the help of Jesus into heroes of their own narratives, conquering the adversities that once held them captive.

After contacting a pastor, a glimmer of hope emerged for Kenny as he was referred to a restoration center in Cincinnati, Ohio. Fueled by this newfound chance for a fresh start, Kenny wasted no time and left for the center the very next day.

The anticipation of transformation and support filled my heart with optimism and a belief that he could overcome the challenges he faced. With the promise of healing and guidance ahead, we both embarked on our journey with renewed determination, knowing that there just might be hope for a brighter future.

Kryptonite

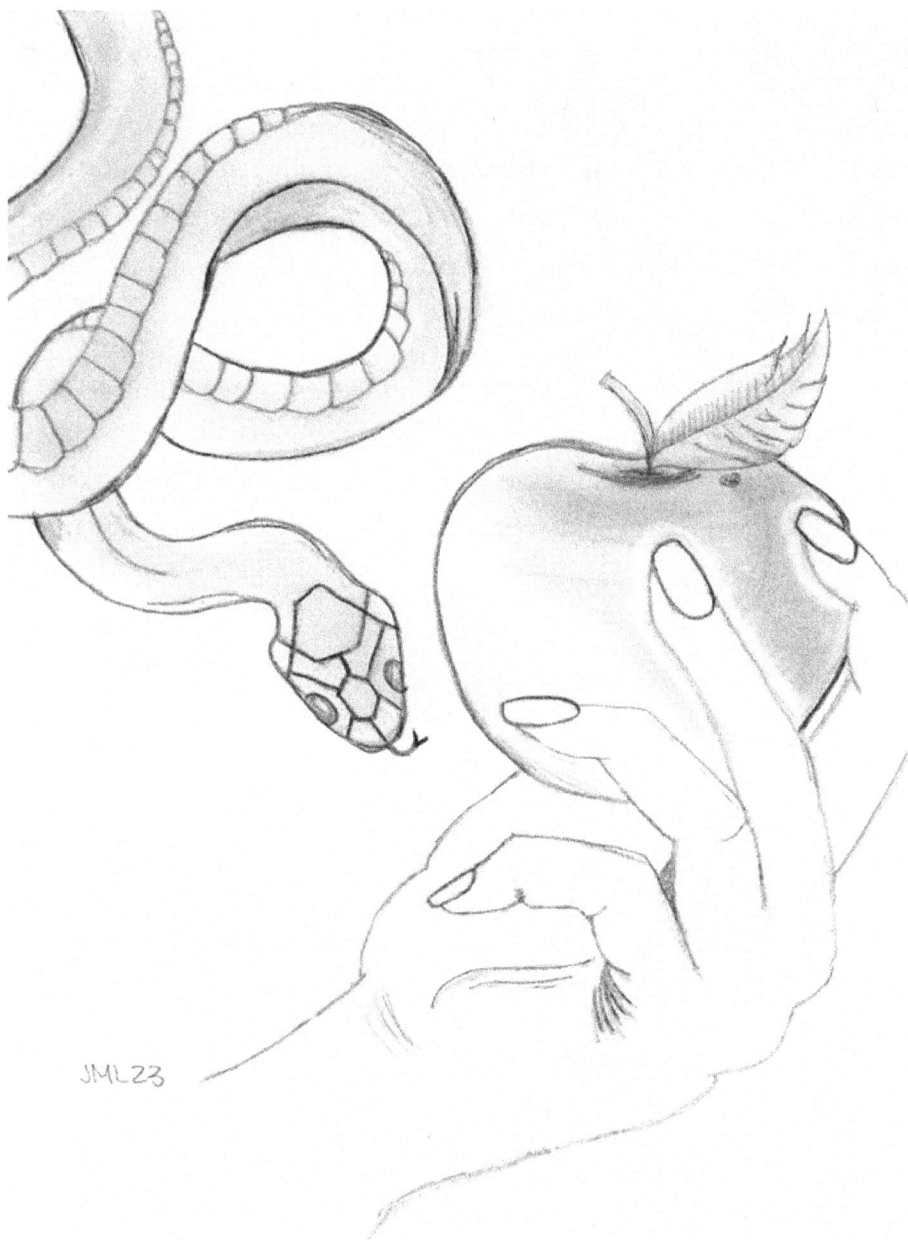

JML23

Redemption

Ruth 3:12

*And now, truly I am one that has the right of redemption, yet there
is one that has the right of redemption who is nearer than I.*

The pastor who referred Kenny to the restoration center was an unwavering support and guidance during that time. I am still in contact with him to this day.

When we were going through this difficult time, this pastor played a pivotal role in our lives. While Kenny was away receiving the care he needed, the pastor continued to be a source of inspiration for me as well.

Recognizing the importance of community service and giving back, the pastor encouraged me to seek volunteer opportunities locally. His belief in the power of service and the potential for positive impact ignited a newfound passion within me. With the pastor's encouragement, I embarked on a search to place myself somewhere to volunteer.

I pondered various avenues that aligned with my passions and interests. I considered nonprofits, environmental initiatives, and many other volunteer organizations. Each option held promise for making a meaningful impact, and I looked forward to finding the perfect fit.

When in the city of Akron, I stumbled on an outreach group "Rahab Ministries." Comprising compassionate volunteers from all walks of life, they dedicated themselves to spreading kindness and healing to those who needed it the most.

Among the many challenges they faced, their most profound mission was to reach out to women caught in the clutches of prostitution and sexual trafficking. These brave volunteers understood that these women's lives were filled with pain, suffering, and loss of hope, and they yearned to make a difference in their lives.

One evening, I joined their team. With their hearts full of empathy and prayers on their lips, the volunteers set out into the streets. As they walked through dimly lit alleys and shadowy corners, they spotted women who appeared weary and downtrodden. With utmost respect, they approached them, offering a warm smile and a gift.

I watched as the women were initially cautious. I am positive they had been mistreated and exploited in the past. However, the genuine sincerity and non-judgmental approach of Rahab's volunteers slowly melted their apprehensions. As conversations unfolded, stories of pain, desperation, and shattered dreams emerged, painting a haunting picture of their past.

I listened attentively, trying to offer a compassionate ear and understanding. Volunteers shared stories of resilience and hope, inspiring the women to believe in their own strength. Through tears and laughter, the walls of isolation began to crumble, replaced by a sense of sisterhood and unity.

In the midst of darkness, a glimmer of hope emerged. Rahab provided information about safe shelters, drop-in houses, counseling services, vocational training programs, and most of all Jesus. They offered a lifeline for those who wished to escape their current circumstances.

As the night progressed, some of the women took the brave step to leave their exploitative situations, seeking help from the resources provided by Rahab. Slowly but surely, as the months went by, I witnessed testimonies and watched many women rebuild their lives, finding the strength to overcome the scars of their past.

Rahab continues their outreach, knowing there are still many women out there who need their support. They recognize that their work is not a quick fix but a testament to the enduring power of Jesus Christ. I enjoyed that season. I made new friends with a diverse group of women whom I still speak with to this day, some volunteers and some that have overcome the throes of sexual exploitation.

Little did I know that Kenny, two days sober, was out in the world evangelizing, sharing his story, his testimonies and offering hope to those in need. It was a beautiful convergence of our paths, as we unknowingly walked the same path of compassion and redemption, even from two very separate angles.

In this unexpected alignment, through scheduled phone calls we discovered that our shared faith and commitment to making a positive impact were guiding forces, weaving our individual journeys into a tapestry of purpose. The revelation of Kenny's evangelizing while being two days sober was a testament to the transformative power of Jesus. It highlighted the redemptive potential within us, even in our moments of brokenness and struggle.

As Kenny continued his journey towards recovery, I stood by his side, extending support and love but only through the grace of God. We wrote letters weekly. We continued to have scheduled calls. I was still very ignorant of drug addiction, but I was learning so many things. I began to navigate the complexities of addiction when he became vulnerable. I again began embracing the lessons of forgiveness, empathy, and the understanding that healing is a continuous process.

In the month of July, (seventh month another God wink) Kenny's return was a momentous occasion, preceded by much discussion and deliberation and numerous heartfelt conversations.

His return home left him homeless, a situation that weighed heavily on our shoulders. However, each morning, I would pick him up from a homeless shelter after dropping Nathaniel off at school. I would drop Kenny off at temp agencies or to do small jobs throughout the day. Through it all, I held onto faith, believing that God would intervene and provide for us in my unwavering faithfulness.

My best friend and her husband ultimately decided to allow him to stay with me and Nathaniel in the cozy apartment I was staying in above their garage. Little did we know that this decision would soon be marked by what we could only describe as an undeniable sign of divine intervention in our lives.

As the days passed, Kenny's presence brought a renewed sense of camaraderie and joy. It felt as though fate had orchestrated every detail, and our hearts were open to the possibility of something extraordinary happening. And extraordinary it was.

Within that seemingly short span of a month, the hand of the Lord moved in ways we could never have imagined. A series of astonishing events unfolded, leaving us in awe of the power of faith and blessings. Miraculously, we found ourselves recipients of divine favor. His employer offered him his job back. A vehicle, which we had been asking for but couldn't afford, was unexpectedly given to us, as if God had conspired to fulfill our dreams.

The most profound blessing came in the form of a new home, a beautiful sanctuary right down the street from my best friend that we never thought we'd have the chance to call our own. It was as if the stars aligned to lead us to this place of comfort and security.

But the miracles didn't stop there. Our church and family of faith showed incredible generosity by providing us with furniture, household items, and even a washer and dryer. These were things that had been sold or stolen during his active drug abuse. Through their support, everything was restored back to us, just as the Lord promised in Joel 2:25: "I will repay you for the years the locusts have eaten." Their kindness truly reflected the spirit of community and restoration that comes from our faith. Throughout this season, we couldn't help but feel that divine providence and how God had played a significant role. Our faith was strengthened, and we couldn't deny the presence of a divine power guiding our path. The experience taught us to trust in the greater plan, even when the future seemed uncertain.

In the midst of life's challenges, it's easy to forget the magic that can happen when we let go and have faith. The return of Kenny brought not just my husband back, but as we reflected on these events, we vowed to carry this sense of gratitude and hope forward, cherishing the course that had changed our lives. Kenny's return was a turning point, reminding me that sometimes, the most extraordinary things happen when we least expect them—all we need to do is trust and have faith in the journey.

As we walked hand in hand, guided by our faith, something extraordinary happened to me. One day, as I sought guidance in prayer, the Lord spoke to me. His voice resonated within my heart, urging me to embark on a mission of compassion and kindness. He said, "Collect blankets, Jody, for there are many who are cold, suffering in poverty, homeless, and trapped in the cycle of addiction."

Inspired by this divine message, Kenny and I founded Revolution Ministries. We wanted a revolt against the darkness, bringing the light of "Jesus Christ" to those struggling in the inner cities.

With newfound purpose, we dedicated ourselves to reaching out to those who desperately needed help, hope, and a warm embrace. Our mission was simple yet profound: to distribute blankets, hygiene supplies, nutritional supplies, and provide support to those stuck in the grips of poverty, homelessness, or drug addiction.

Kenny and I, with a renewed sense of purpose and conviction, embarked on our ministry journey, confident that we were finally aligned with God's will. Our shared faith and passion for serving others filled our hearts with joy and anticipation at what God would do next.

In our quest to discover a life verse that would guide and inspire us, we diligently searched the scriptures and finally found it in Zachariah 11:7. This particular verse held a profound significance for us. Of course, the significance of the numbers but mostly serving as a guiding light on our journey through life.

Its words resonated deep within our hearts, offering wisdom into the calling the Lord had put on our lives. As we embraced this verse, we found comfort in knowing that we had a source of guidance and inspiration to lean on, helping us to stay true to our values and purpose as we walk through life's diverse paths.

Zachariah 11:7: "And I will feed the flock of slaughter, even you, O poor of the flock. And I took unto me two staves; the one I called Beauty, and the other I called Bands; and I fed the flock."

Redemption

JML23

Trials Just Like Job

---◆◇◆---

Job 9:35

Then I would speak [my defense] and not fear Him; but I am not like that in myself.

Amidst the blessings of this new chapter, new trials would be exposed. Kenny and I were overjoyed to find out I was pregnant once more, a glimmer of hope after our previous challenges. However, our excitement turned to concern when the first ultrasound revealed a blighted ovum—a situation where the gestational sac develops, but the embryo does not form or stops growing very early on. This unexpected outcome was disheartening, as we had experienced a similar disappointment before. Still, we clung to our faith and the belief that life's trials are a part of a larger plan. While past experiences had taught us about setbacks, this time felt different. We persevered through the heartache, and for the first time, we managed to navigate this difficult path with the strength and trust in God that we had been striving for all along.

Then came my ex-husband's unexpected move to file for custodial parenting. This shattered my heart. The emotional toll was immense, and I grappled with feelings of fear, sadness, and uncertainty. Nevertheless, we leaned on our faith more than ever, seeking strength in prayer and the support of other believers of faith. Though the road ahead seemed daunting, we trusted that

God's plan would ultimately guide us through the storm, holding onto the belief that His love would carry us through more turbulent times.

As the court proceedings unfolded, my heart was broken at the thought of potentially losing my son. The bond we shared was profound, and the idea of being separated from him seemed unbearable. Every word spoken during the hearing echoed in my mind, and the emotional weight of the situation was overwhelming. But in the midst of my pain, I clung to my faith, finding strength in the belief that God's plan was at work, even in the darkest moments. Just like Job's unwavering faith during his trials, I held on to hope, trusting that somehow, this painful chapter would lead to a greater purpose and bring about a resolution that would be in the best interest of my son.

During the court hearings, I often felt deeply persecuted, especially while navigating discussions surrounding our outreach activities and sharing the message of Jesus. The atmosphere was tense, and it seemed like our intentions were misunderstood and misrepresented. In the courtroom, we then found ourselves under intense scrutiny over Kenny's relapses and for involving my son in outreach activities. Our friend Jason had also moved from South Carolina and was living with us to help with ministry work. He and Nathaniel had formed a great bond, but this was also misinterpreted, as the judge made the assumption that Jason was homeless and that he had been invited into our home.

During this time, I ruminated on the events surrounding Jesus' crucifixion. I felt an overwhelming connection with him. Despite the crowd's cries to crucify him, I empathize with his unwavering love and compassion even in the face of hostility. It was disheartening to see how just like him, Kenny and I were being accused and misrepresented by my ex-husband's lawyer. Jesus remained steadfast in his teachings of forgiveness and understanding. I still don't understand the full capacity of the trial Jesus endured.

The profound injustice he endured at the hands of those who misunderstood him, even those who had witnessed his miracles. This made me reflect on the importance of standing firm in one's beliefs, even when faced with adversity. His selfless sacrifice and willingness to bear the burden of false accusations were a testament to his divine nature and unwavering faith in his mission. Was that not our calling also?

During those tumultuous times, I found comfort in knowing that Jesus' teachings continue to inspire countless people to embrace love, empathy, and kindness. His life serves as a reminder that even in difficult moments, there is a glimmer of hope and a path towards redemption. Witnessing his journey made me cherish the power of resilience and unwavering devotion to my higher purpose, despite the challenges and misrepresentations that may come my way.

Although clearly just accusations, I understood the concerns of my ex-husband.

The situation seemed to draw disapproval from the judge, which led us to bring in our own character witnesses, multiple friends and pastors. Despite the negative perception, our primary aim was always to instill values of compassion and empathy in my son. We firmly believed that exposing him to the significance of the work of recovery that Kenny continued, outreach, and kindness would contribute to a more compassionate and interconnected individual to society.

Throughout the legal proceedings, our character witnesses testified to the positive impact our efforts had on my son, highlighting the meaningful difference he made in the lives of those we served and with this we included the safety measures and guidelines that were always in place when he was with us. They also explained when Kenny was in active addiction it was never done in our home and that I removed Nathaniel and left during his two previous relapses. The experience was emotionally taxing, as I felt targeted for practicing my faith and advocating for what I believed in. Throughout the hearings, I found strength in my convictions, knowing that standing up for what I held dear was worth enduring the hardships we encountered in the pursuit of religious freedom and understanding.

At the end of the hearing, Nathaniel found himself in an important conversation with the judge presiding over his custody case. She invited him into her chambers privately to ask him questions and his perspective. During their discussion, Nathaniel bravely expressed his desire to spend more time with his father. He also shared his excitement about attending his first school again if this change were to happen. After carefully considering Nathaniel's wishes and his father's suitability, the judge ultimately granted making my ex-husband the custodial parent. While this decision was about to change the lives of all involved, the judge believed it was in Nathaniel's best interest to explore a new chapter in his life.

The circumstances left me uncertain about whether I had accurately interpreted the Lord's guidance. Although the judge stated her decision wasn't influenced by me not being a good mother, but rather by Nathaniel's testimony, I still carried a sense of responsibility, wondering if my choices had led to this situation.

The finalization of the court proceedings and my ex-husband taking my son shattered my life. The sense of loss and heartache overwhelmed me during those weeks. However, amidst the changes, I turned to the book of Job again and again for wisdom and found encouragement in its messages of perseverance and faith. Reading about Job's trials and how his friends treated him further resonated with my own struggles. Despite facing severe afflictions, Job's friends and family initially offered him support, but as his suffering continued, they began to doubt and blame him. I remember one statement from a friend that still resonates in me at my core. "If you continue to do outreach and stay with someone who is in recovery, you deserve to lose your son." This parallel helped me reflect on the importance of true compassion and understanding during difficult times, reinforcing the significance of the genuine support from those around us.

As I sought the Lord, I saw the resemblance to the divine story of God, who made the ultimate sacrifice by giving up his only son, Jesus, to fulfill a higher purpose. Just as God had a grand plan for Jesus, it seemed that my own life and that of Nathaniel was guided by a greater calling. Throughout this season, I encountered moments of sacrifice and challenges, just like how God, Job and eventually Mary the mother of Jesus did.

These experiences shaped me into the person I am today and prepared me to continue to walk in my destined path despite fear and emotional pain. In my heart I knew that I had the most impressionable years with Nathaniel. I was able to instill in him the truths and foundations of Jesus. I was able to show him love and how to overcome it with determination and I tried to encourage his giftings. As God's purpose unfolded again and again over time, so did mine, and through it all, I embraced my calling with God's strength. For when we are weak, he is strong.

My life's resemblance to God is only meant to illustrate the profound wisdom and lessons that can be found in divine narratives, and it reminds me of the resilience and significance of our own journeys in fulfilling our unique destinies.

Even though Nathaniel had moved in with his father to attend school, our bond with him remained strong. Our relationship with Nathaniel transcended. Although I felt his absence, we kept in touch with daily calls and midweek and weekend visits. We remained connected on a deeper level. Despite the change in his living situation, Nathaniel expressed a strong desire to continue being part of outreach. Our weekends together demonstrated his commitment to our shared endeavors and the sense of belonging he found within our community. His involvement and dedication were truly heartening, reflecting the lasting impact we had on him.

Through it all, we held onto the belief that Jesus was working everything out for our good. Our experiences, though painful and challenging, became the steppingstones that led not only Kenny and I but Nathaniel to a deeper understanding of grace, compassion, and the resilience of the human spirit.

In the Bible, the story of Job is a profound example of enduring trials and receiving blessings. Job was a righteous man, known for his faithfulness and devotion to God. However, he faced severe trials and tribulations that tested his faith to the core.

Job's trials began when he lost his wealth, possessions, and even his children in a series of devastating events. Despite this immense suffering, he remained steadfast in his faith and refused to curse God. As if that was not enough, he was afflicted with painful sores, adding physical agony to his emotional turmoil.

In the midst of his trials, Job's friends offered various explanations for his suffering, assuming he must have done something to deserve such punishment. However, Job maintained his innocence and questioned God's purpose in his suffering, seeking understanding.

After enduring these trials, Job's faith and resilience were rewarded with blessings beyond measure. God restored his health, wealth, and gave him a new family, even more abundant than before. Job's steadfastness and unwavering faith led to a deeper understanding of God's sovereignty and a profound spiritual growth.

In my own trial, I found many similarities with Job's experiences. Enduring hardships can be incredibly challenging, but holding onto your faith and remaining steadfast can lead to a greater appreciation of life's blessings once the trial subsides. Just like Job, I prayed my perseverance might bring about unexpected blessings and growth in ways I might not anticipate. I found my trust in the process and tried to remember that trials can often lead to profound spiritual transformation.

Trials Just Like Job

JML22

A Revolution Begins

Zechariah 11:7

So I became the shepherd of the flock marked for slaughter, paying attention to the oppressed of the flock. I took two staff naming one "Pleasant" and the other one "Union" - and then I pastured the flock.

In the years that followed, our lives became purposeful with Revolution Ministries, where Kenny and I channeled our collective pain and experiences into a mission of healing and transformation. We recognized the power of our stories to offer hope and encouragement to those who were walking similar paths of addiction, loss, and trauma.

One of our mottos was we feed people physically and then that gives us the opportunity to feed them spirituality with prayer and sharing the Gospel.

In the promise given to us, there was a provision that brought immense blessings to our journey. It all began with the pastor that referred Kenny to Cincinnati. It opened so many paths for new opportunities.

Through this connection, we were gifted 5000 FEMA blankets, a gesture that provided warmth and comfort to those in need. Excitingly, we also received an invitation to join his team on a mission trip to the inner-city streets of Detroit. Filled with a sense of purpose and eagerness to make a positive impact, we accepted the call to lend a helping hand to those in need. Our hearts were open, ready to embrace the journey that awaited us and eager to contribute to the mission's efforts in feeding, clothing, and offering prayers to hundreds of people.

The kindness didn't end there; our churches united to rally behind us, generously donating hygiene products and various items, amplifying the impact of our mission. Among the many supporters, a remarkable woman named Sarah stepped forward and touched our hearts with her immense generosity. Sarah selflessly donated over 6000 brand new t-shirts, providing not just clothing but a sense of dignity to those we served.

The shirts donated were branded with distinctive designs or logos. As we drove through Akron, we could often easily identify the individuals we had encountered based on whether they were wearing those unique shirts. It created a sense of connection and awareness, knowing that the shirts served as a visual representation of our encounters with people who had been prayed for or provided with necessary assistance during our outreach efforts.

Sarah's contribution went far beyond material donations. For many years she remained an integral part of our lives, extending her support beyond the realm of charity. She served as a mentor to us in ministry, guiding us on our spiritual path and empowering us to make a difference in the lives of others. Additionally, Sarah offered counsel and guidance to Kenny, becoming a trusted confidante and friend.

Sarah's presence on our journey was a beautiful reminder of the power of compassion and human connection. Her unwavering support, both in material contributions and personal guidance, enriched our lives and strengthened our mission to help those in need.

During the peak of an opiate crisis, Revolution Ministries actively participated in community meetings and events to address the pressing and devastating impact of opioid addiction. We dedicated ourselves to helping individuals struggling with addictions.

In response to the crisis, these community meetings served as vital platforms where we could collectively devise comprehensive strategies to combat the crisis head-on.

Engaging directly with the community during these meetings allowed us to gain valuable insights into the specific challenges and needs faced by those grappling with opioid addiction. We used this information to advocate for more accessible treatment options, spread awareness about the resources available, and emphasize the importance of destigmatizing addiction.

Amidst these challenging times, I feel our unwavering commitment to helping individuals find hope and recovery remained resolute. We leveraged the collective expertise and resources of the community to implement targeted interventions and support initiatives, supporting those already affected.

Through our active involvement in these community meetings during the opiate crisis, we showcased our dedication to driving positive change and instilled a sense of unity in the fight against addiction. As a result, collectively everyone played a significant role in fostering a stronger, more compassionate community that worked together to combat the crisis and provide hope to those seeking a way out of the darkness of addiction. Our impact reverberated not only through the lives of individuals we directly helped but also through the communities we served. I believe this left a legacy of compassion, hope, and transformation in our surrounding city.

Together, Kenny and I witnessed the transformative power of faith, compassion, and prayer in our own lives and in the lives of others. In this ongoing journey, we continued to learn and grow. We understood that our trials and triumphs were not in vain, but rather vehicles for growth, empathy, understanding, and the potential to inspire change.

Through it all, Jesus remained at the center, guiding our steps, and working through our pain to bring forth the fruit of our obedience. He took our brokenness and turned it into a story of hope.

In embracing our own healing and supporting others in their journey, we discovered there is always a divine plan at work. Our pain became a platform for compassion, our struggles a catalyst for change, and our faith an unyielding source of strength.

Equipped with love and a steadfast determination, we set out into the world, seeking to bring light to the darkest corners of society. A REVOLUTION of love. Together, we forged connections with local shelters, addiction recovery centers, and community organizations, offering our time, resources, and most importantly, our understanding.

On chilly nights, we ventured into the streets, laden with blankets and provisions. We approached individuals huddled in doorways, seeking shelter beneath tattered blankets, tent communities, and local parks and extended a hand of empathy.

We fed people in parking garages, we sent people to treatment, we spent countless hours talking and praying with people struggling. We paid for bus tickets to get individuals to treatment. Jenn and Ed continued to walk beside us in their unyielding support. With each encounter, we listened to stories, sharing in individuals' pain and struggles. We offered warmth, both in the form of physical necessities and the warmth of human connection.

During that time, during a family night, Nathaniel and I noticed a woman sitting by the doors at a gas station. When we walked by she asked for help. She said she was hungry, and she really wanted a sandwich but that she only had $.75. I offered to buy her whatever she needed if she would allow me and my husband to pray for her. We prayed for her and took the opportunity to talk to her about seeking recovery and treatment.

Despite her stunning blue eyes, it was evident and very apparent she was struggling with substance abuse and going through a challenging time. We shared Kenny's story of recovery and the transformative power of seeking treatment.

She wept as we asked her if she would agree to treatment. She quickly responded with a simple yes. I was overwhelmed with her decision. After many attempts that evening, we couldn't get her a bus ticket to send her to a treatment facility. Our only choice was to take her to a local homeless shelter. But within an hour they called stating they couldn't accommodate her detoxing situation as it could trigger others in recovery. We decided our only other choice to keep her safe was to take her to the hospital in hopes of getting her help.

I assisted her while she was being admitted but unfortunately, when we returned the next day, she had discharged herself, and was gone.

During our initial conversation, she had bravely shared her painful experience of being sexually trafficked, making her very vulnerable. Her story touched me deeply, and I felt compelled to intercede for her in ways I had never done before. I spoke to other groups, hoping that they might have contact or interactions with her, and if I couldn't reach her directly, I fervently prayed that someone else would step in to offer help and support. Her situation moved me to tears many nights, and my heart ached for her well-being and safety.

Weeks after our initial encounter, Another outreach team notified me they had the fortune of meeting her again. They kindly provided her with our contact number, and she reached out to us while preparing to return home to Massachusetts to enter treatment. Knowing she was about to depart, she requested to see us one last time before her journey.

Filled with compassion, we swiftly gathered some clean clothes, snacks, and a Bible. It was a small gesture, but we hoped it would bring her comfort on her bus journey home.

As we bid her farewell, there was a sense of gratitude and relief in her eyes. Although our encounter was brief, knowing that we could make a difference, even in a small way, made this one experience profoundly rewarding to me. We prayed for her safe travels and hoped that our paths might cross again someday.

Eight and a half years later, I'm still in touch with her, and she is clean and sober with a beautiful son who is three. Her transformation encourages me, and it reaffirms my belief that reaching just one person through ministry is worth it. This is just one of the many testimonies that I have encountered. Her willingness to seek treatment played a crucial role in her successful recovery, and it remains an inspiring story for me to remember.

Revolution Ministries became a collective force of compassion, an embodiment of love in action. Our team expanded, enabling us to broaden our reach, co-labor with other teams, and touch more lives.

We sought to empower those we encountered. We connected individuals with vital resources, and we encouraged them to believe in their inherent worth, reminding them that their past did not define their future.

Through Revolution Ministries, I witnessed miracles unfold. I saw individuals find Jesus, overcome addiction, find stable housing, and reconnect with their families. We celebrated stories of hope and restoration, knowing that our efforts through Jesus, no matter how small, began to make a difference.

Our journey together had transformed not only the lives of others but also our own. Kenny's own experience with recovery became his platform helping those who were still struggling, while my faith grew stronger as I witnessed the resurrection power in full motion.

As the years passed, Revolution Ministries became my unyielding belief in the power of redemption. Through that first simple act of obedience, collecting blankets, we built a community of care, proving that every individual deserves a second chance to be seen, valued, and loved.

And so, our story continued, one blanket, one prayer, one heart at a time, as we strived to create a world where no one was left behind.

Revolution Ministries emerged because of Kenny overcoming his own trials with addiction that once bound him by the suffocating chains of drugs. As we embarked on this journey together, our vision was clear. It was plain—to create a community that understood the struggles individuals and families faced and to offer unwavering support to those seeking help. We knew firsthand the challenges of addiction and believed that by sharing our story and experiences as a unit, we could inspire others to embark on their own journeys of recovery.

Revolution Ministries offered a comprehensive approach to healing, tailoring our support to meet the unique needs of each individual seeking help. Kenny and I ensured that those who sought assistance would find the guidance and tools needed to confront the underlying issues fueling addiction.

Our outreach program aimed to destigmatize addiction, fostering a safe space for healing and growth. We wanted everyone who walked into our life to know that they were not judged for their past, but rather celebrated for their courage to seek a better future.

As the days turned into weeks and months, the impact of Revolution Ministries on the lives of those we served became undeniable. We witnessed remarkable transformations, individuals breaking free from addiction's grasp and finding a renewed sense of purpose and hope.

In the embrace of Revolution Ministries, our team created a second family—a family that uplifted, encouraged, and celebrated the successes of all members. Together, we stood united against the darkness of addiction, illuminating the path to redemption, hope, and a brighter future.

As I reflect on the journey with Revolution Ministries, I am filled with gratitude for the opportunity to make a difference in the lives of others. Kenny and I knew that it was the dedication of our team and the support of our community and other organizations that paved the way for healing and transformation in our city.

Kenny often described Revolution Ministries as a powerful revolt against the darkness that had engulfed our community. He likened it to a radiant dawn breaking through a long night, bringing a renewed sense of hope and purpose to those lost in the shadows.

As I think about it now, our group, just as a firefly's glow, multiplied with each new addition. The more people who joined the movement, the more people who overcame, and the stronger our collective voice became, pushing back against the oppressive forces of hopelessness.

Kenny envisioned Revolution Ministries as a gathering of torchbearers, each carrying a flame of hope and dedication to shine brightly in the face of adversity. Together, he knew we formed an unyielding wall against the darkness, fostering a sense of belonging and empowerment in the lives of those we touched.

Our act of revolt against the darkness wasn't violent or aggressive; it was a peaceful uprising of hearts and minds, standing against the injustices and hardships that plagued our community. Revolution Ministries was like a symphony of light in a once-silent and bleak night, uniting together with a common purpose and a shared vision of a brighter future.

We always saw the potential for a transformative revolution, where the darkness would be dispelled by the illuminating power of Jesus.

It's true that the impact we have on others is often hard to quantify. The ripples of our actions can spread far beyond what we realize. While we may never fully grasp the extent of the people we've helped, the knowledge that we've made a positive difference in a few has been a huge source of fulfillment for me. As I look forward to a moment of personal fulfillment and being in glory, this feeling of accomplishment has served as a reminder of the few positive achievements we have made along the way. These accomplishments would not have been possible without the guidance and inspiration drawn from Jesus.

A Revolution Begins

Jesus My King

Job 19:25

But as for me, I know that my Redeemer lives. In the end, he will stand upon the earth.

Kenny was always a compassionate and driven individual. From the day I met him he found his true calling in helping others. Having overcome his own battle with addiction, Kenny knew firsthand the challenges faced by those in recovery. Determined to make a difference, he decided to start his own power washing and contracting business and provide meaningful employment opportunities to individuals in recovery.

Kenny and I prayed about what God wanted him to name his company. After much thought Kenny decided to name the company "JMK" for Jesus My King. His logo then included, "JMK making all things new." I still chuckle remembering a conversation we had after he registered his business with the state. He charmingly but arrogantly explained the Lord had given him a great revelation.

I was excited to hear about it. Kenny was true to his cryptic and analytical nature, even when sharing the profound revelations he believed God had bestowed upon him. His interactions were characterized by a unique blend of intellect and spirituality, making his insights all the more captivating.

When Kenny spoke of the revelations he received from God, he did so in a manner that left me pondering and contemplating my own understanding of the divine. As a result, his words often carried layers of meaning, challenging me to explore beyond the surface and seek my own connections with God and often left me studying scripture.

Kenny's ability to present complex spiritual concepts in a cryptic yet compelling way created an aura of reverence around him. I couldn't help but feel a sense of awe and wonder, as if glimpsing into a realm where the spiritual and intellectual converged. His revelations were not only a testament to his profound understanding but also a reminder of the boundless depth of God's wisdom. He taught me many times to embrace the mystery and complexity that life and spirituality had to offer.

And so I sat there waiting, hands crossed in anticipation like a little child. He was silent.

I became impatient, and I began teasingly saying, "Tell me. Tell Me, Kenneth. Tell me. Tell Me." I remember sighing, and becoming frustrated I shouted, "Tell me already!" He laughed his very distinct laugh which at times sounded half like Woody Woodpecker and said, "The lord showed me Jesus was King," and that his business name also stood for Jody Married Kenny.

He laughed, I laughed, and we continued to laugh. I know it may sound silly to you but as I reminisce Kenny's depth, charm, and humor were the captivating character traits that drew me towards him and made me fall in love with him. Sometimes over and over again.

His ability to delve into profound and deep conversations, his genuine charm that made everyone around him feel at ease, and his witty sense of humor that could light up any room were all irresistible qualities.

Throughout our journey together, these traits became the foundation of our bond, as they enriched our connection and made every moment together more meaningful. Kenny's deepness inspired thought-provoking discussions not only with me but in others, his charm nurtured our emotional intimacy, and his humor brought joy and laughter even during challenging times. It was these exceptional qualities that fueled my determination to fight for our marriage, knowing that with him, life would always be an adventure filled with overcoming challenges, of course, but with a lot of love and laughter in the midst.

So, armed with a donated power washer, his skills as a contractor, and a heart full of empathy, he embarked on another mission. He mentored and trained men in recovery. He understood that steady employment played a crucial role in the recovery process, offering stability, purpose, and a sense of accomplishment.

During this time, he also dedicated his weekends to mentoring at a recovery agency. In addition to his regular commitments, he ensured that the men had meaningful and "Sober Saturdays" as we called them at our home. These weekends were filled with a sense of camaraderie and purpose as we gathered the men, provided a meal, shared in scripture, packed outreach bags for those in need, and enjoyed movies as a family unit. His guidance and support had a positive impact on many lives, fostering a sense of community and helping individuals on their journey to recovery.

Every weekend, as this group of young men would come to our home, they also became eager to attend church with us on Sundays. Over time, they became an integral part of our family, and their warm affection led them to lovingly call me "mom" and they all considered Nathaniel a little brother. It was a heartwarming experience for me to witness their genuine transformation, not just in their journey with Jesus but also in the deep bond we all formed. Together we created cherished memories that would forever remain etched in my heart. I find it overwhelming to still get phone calls from them occasionally when they are in the midst of struggle. It is such a blessing to me that at times they still seek counsel, encouragement, and prayers from me. Sometimes they also call to just share something they have overcome or have accomplished. These moments I see God's hand in all the things we ever did, and it's a reminder that unconditional love brings forth long and lasting fruit.

Many were intrigued by the opportunity to not only earn a living but also work in a supportive environment where their unique journeys were understood and valued. Many individuals, determined to turn their lives around, eagerly approached Kenny, seeking employment.

Kenny meticulously selected each candidate, considering their skills, dedication, and commitment to their recovery. He believed in giving everyone a fair chance, recognizing that second chances could lead to a life change.

He often said that if you can change someone's mindset an ⅛ of a degree, and they received just a slight revelation of Jesus, you've done your job. God would always bring someone behind us to water the grounds we plowed.

As Kenny's contracting business expanded, he took on a variety of projects, spanning from home renovations to community improvement initiatives at local outreach centers. His dedication to his work resulted in stunning spaces and a positive influence on Akron. Kenny's commitment to professionalism, reliability, and outstanding craftsmanship earned him a strong reputation. Interestingly, his cousin, who was fresh out of prison, became his partner.

It was inspiring to witness his cousin's journey unfold before my eyes. I watched with admiration as he dedicated himself to hard work, steadily building his path towards success. Seeing him become engaged marked a beautiful chapter of his life, a testament to his commitment and love. Then he embarked on the journey of starting his own family. It was heartwarming to observe the bonds he was forming and the new responsibilities he was embracing.

Local residents including prosecutors and judges began seeking out Kenny's services, not just because of his outstanding work ethic and performance but also because they believed in supporting the cause and giving back to the community.

His business became a symbol of second chances and the belief that everyone deserved an opportunity to heal and thrive. This brought deeper meaning to Jesus My King and making all things new.

Kenny met a man just out of recovery who began to work with him on jobs. Over time, they developed a strong working relationship, tackling various jobs together. Kenny admired the man's determination and believed in his ability to overcome past struggles. As a result, when the man faced a relapse, Kenny didn't give up on him. Instead, we supported him and offered to send him to treatment, offering him second and even third chances to turn his life around. Kenny was resolute on the potential he had.

JMK became very expansive, and I too began to work with my husband. Cleaning and painting, going on estimates, and enjoying the favor the Lord had given us.

The favor of the Lord was undeniably present during this time, as I not only experienced His blessings in various aspects of my life but also relished the joy of having my husband fully sober and by my side.

Working together with him felt like a harmonious dance, where our strengths complemented each other seamlessly. The favor we witnessed seemed to amplify our collaboration, making our efforts more fruitful and rewarding. The Lord's favor became a guiding force that brought us closer, deepening our bond and strengthening our love.

The joy of being in each other's company, both in our personal life and professional endeavors, was immeasurable. With the Lord's favor evident in every step we took, we found contentment, cherishing the blessings of partnership and the bliss of knowing that the path we walked was divinely orchestrated.

Jesus is My King

JML 23

Superman's Demise

Isaiah 57:1

The righteous perisheth, and no man layeth it to heart: and merciful men are taken away, none considering that the righteous is taken away from the evil to come.

Kenny began struggling with pain and life took an unfortunate turn for us. Kenny underwent testing and was diagnosed with CPT, Carpal Tunnel Syndrome. The pain became noticeable to me even after steroid injections as he constantly walked around holding or massaging his wrist.

We made the decision for him to undergo carpal tunnel surgery, causing him to experience increased pain and discomfort after surgery. The doctor offered a short dose of pain medicine unbeknownst to me. Throughout his five years of sobriety, in any medical situation we were vulnerable with doctors about his past drug abuse with opiates and the need to have non-narcotic pain medicine to remain in recovery. Looking back, I know this was a detrimental mistake on many parties including Kenny's.

The man whom Kenny employed and had shown unwavering faith in, along with others began providing him with opiates on job sites, initially with the intention of alleviating Kenny's pain. These actions, although driven by a desire to help, added to and ultimately put Kenny's well-being and recovery at risk.

Tragically in 2020 and after five years of sobriety Kenny faced a devastating setback, leading him back into the grips of the darkness of opiate addiction. In addition to the challenges we faced with Kenny's relapse, the world was thrust into the midst of a global crisis—the COVID pandemic. The sudden onset of the pandemic brought with it a wave of uncertainty, fear, and disruption to our lives. It was during this trying time that Kenny's faith began to waver.

The weight of the relapse and the overwhelming impact of the pandemic took a toll on Kenny's spiritual journey. He began having panic attacks. The combination of personal struggles, continued use of opiates, and the collective uncertainty surrounding the pandemic tested his faith.

During the pandemic, my husband's concern for my health, given my work in healthcare, overwhelmed him. He dedicated countless hours to finding sanitizer and Lysol, ensuring I had the necessary precautions to stay safe.

As I came downstairs late one night, I was taken aback to find my husband weeping on the floor. He tearfully revealed that he was struggling, that he believed it was God who had awakened me at that precise moment. Despite my previous efforts as an intercessor and going to great lengths to support him, it became evident that seeking the guidance of Jesus and wise mentors was essential in navigating this challenging situation. My support was not enough.

On that fateful night, as my husband became vulnerable and shared his loss of faith, he earnestly pleaded for mine. It sparked a cascade of thoughts and emotions that led to a profound and transformative realization. As I sat there, listening intently to his words, I felt an internal struggle brewing within me.

For so long, I had carried the weight of trying to be a savior, believing that if I could fix everyone's problems and save them from their hardships, I could somehow make their lives better.

But as he spoke, I began to see the fallacy in my thinking. I understood that I was not Jesus, and I could not bear the burden of saving others.

I was merely a human, with my own limitations and imperfections. It was a revelation that shook me to the core, and yet, paradoxically, it liberated me from the unrealistic expectations I had imposed upon myself.

In that moment of clarity, I realized that trying to be a savior was not only futile but also detrimental to both myself and those around me. It prevented others from taking responsibility for their actions and growth, while I, in turn, neglected my own needs and well-being.

Accepting this truth was not easy, as I had been here before. I had to learn to let go of the compulsion to fix everything and everyone. Instead, I needed to focus on being a compassionate and supportive presence in their lives, encouraging them to find their own strength and resilience.

In the days that followed, I learned to embrace my vulnerabilities and recognize that it was okay not to have all the answers. I allowed myself to lean on others for support when needed, acknowledging that seeking help didn't make me weak, but rather, human.

As I learned to release the need to be a savior, I found a newfound sense of freedom and authenticity in my relationships. The pressure to rescue others lifted, and I could connect with them on a deeper, more genuine level. We shared our joys and sorrows, navigating life's challenges together without the weight of my unrealistic expectations.

That night was a turning point in my life—an awakening that reshaped my perspective and approach to relationships. It taught me the power of humility, acceptance, and compassion for both myself and others. While I couldn't be a savior, I realized that by embracing my humanity and loving others unconditionally, I could make a profound and lasting impact on their lives. And in doing so, I would embark on a journey of growth and fulfillment that would ultimately bring me closer to my true self.

Over the next month, in my earnest efforts to support Kenny, I consistently encouraged him to seek Jesus and reminded him of the profound wisdom found in seeking counsel. Drawing from the scriptures, I shared with him the powerful message of Proverbs 11:14, which highlights the importance of seeking guidance from a multitude of counselors. I emphasized how connecting with Jesus and immersing oneself in His teachings could bring unparalleled clarity, strength, and purpose during his challenging moments.

Together, we explored the words of the Bible. I prayed with him every morning before work. I anointed his boots. We discussed scripture and its timeless lessons and the comforting reassurance that Jesus is always there to offer grace.

While I wholeheartedly wanted to save him from his struggles, I humbly acknowledged that the power to heal and provide ultimate salvation lay with his surrender and Jesus alone. Thus, I prayed fervently for Kenny's well-being, hoping that he would find peace and support through seeking Jesus' divine wisdom and guidance. Understanding that genuine salvation and transformation come from a personal connection with Jesus, I stood by Kenny, reassuring him and believing in the transformative power of faith.

On Good Friday I eagerly awaited my husband's return from work. I had spoken to him, and he had stated that he had one estimate before he would return home as we had planned and discussed going to the grocery store together to buy food for our Easter dinner. However, as the hours passed, and he never arrived, worry and anxiety consumed me. I had that fleeting flutter in my chest. Frantically, I called his phone, and it went directly to voicemail. I reached out to everyone I knew, desperately searching for any clue about his whereabouts. In my desperation, I sought the help of intercessors, hoping their prayers would guide him back to safety. Amidst the uncertainty, two of our friends arrived at the house, and together, we embarked on a mission to locate him. We combed through all the properties where he might have been working, our hearts heavy with concern for his well-being. The night seemed to stretch on forever as we clung to hope and prayed for his safe return.

At eight o'clock the following morning, I finally received a call from him, and my heart sank as I heard the guilt and shame in his voice. He shared the news that he had relapsed and would be coming home shortly. The weight of his struggle was evident, and I knew that this was a challenging moment for him.

Often, the best ways to respond to an addict can have the breathtaking capacity to drown those who love them with guilt, grief, self-doubt, and of course, resistance. Could I have done something different?

Loving an addict in any capacity can be one of the loneliest places in the world. It's easy to feel judged for support you give or don't give to the addict. Unless someone has been in battle armor beside you, fighting the fight, being brought to their knees, with their heart-broken and their will tested, they will never understand. As my husband embarked on his detox journey, I began to witness the true demons he had been battling all along.

Let me tell you, watching a loved one go through detox is an emotionally exhausting experience, not for the faint of heart. Witnessing their struggle to break free from addiction, while grappling with the physical and psychological challenges of withdrawal, can be heart-wrenching. The rollercoaster of emotions, from hope to fear and frustration, can leave one feeling powerless and overwhelmed. The road to recovery demands immense resilience and compassion from both the individual and their supportive circle. Although I had worked in the recovery arena for over five years, I did not know that detox could be severe, ranging from nausea, vomiting, sweating, and anxiety to more intense effects like hallucinations.

This was an experience I had never shared with him before, as he had always sought treatment in a facility in the past. Watching him confront his struggles head-on, I gained a deeper understanding of the immense strength and resilience recovery possessed. It was a challenging and eye-opening time for me.

Over the next two weeks, I observed a troubling pattern in his behavior. At first, I believed he was making progress, but soon it became apparent that his heart remained unrepentant, and his moods swung drastically.

Concerned for his well-being, I urged him to seek professional treatment, as well as guidance from mentors and pastors, hoping they could provide the support and insight he needed. Despite my insistence, he chose not to take these steps, leaving me deeply worried about his emotional and spiritual state.

I prayed for weeks and then I made a decision to contact volunteers letting them know we would be ceasing to do outreach due to his relapse. When I made the difficult decision to cancel outreach, I found myself facing significant disdain from other members of the team. The emotions ran high as many had invested time, effort, and passion into our project. I suppose, some may have struggled to comprehend the impact of Kenny's relapse on our initiative. Navigating these strong reactions was undoubtedly challenging for me.

I also started having bouts of fear. My fear often revolved around the potential loss of material items due to the financial strain caused by his addiction. Additionally, there was a constant feeling of dread at the risk of his overdose and the potential for death. This fear stemmed from the uncertainty of how addiction might progress in my husband's life and the devastating impact it could have on everything we worked so hard to restore.

Again I felt judged and misunderstood.

It was a difficult but necessary decision for everyone involved. Outreach programs are crucial in providing support and assistance to those in need, but in the case of his relapse, it was important to prioritize his well-being and focus on addressing his underlying issues contributing to his own struggles. By temporarily stepping back from outreach efforts, the hope was to allow him the time and space to prioritize his own recovery and seek the help and treatment he needed. With the loss of his own faith and his relapse he would not be able to accomplish God's call until he started again on the journey of his own healing.

With each passing day, I continued to navigate the ebb and flow of my own faith, recognizing that it is a journey marked by both mountaintop moments and moments of doubt. I sought many friends, leaders, and mentors during this time.

As Kenny's addiction took hold, I faced immense struggles trying to separate myself from the situation. After an argument over his continued use of drugs, he asked me to leave. The weight of it all became too heavy to bear, and three months later on June 28, I made the difficult decision to move out, seeking safety, some distance, and clarity. Never with the intention of divorce, but for my own healing.

Helping someone struggling with drug or alcohol addiction is often a long and heartbreaking journey. At times, it can be so overwhelming that ignoring the situation may seem like an easier solution. But sweeping the issue under the rug can be more damaging to you, and the person you're concerned about. As painful as it may be, it's important that you take the time to encourage the person to get help and support them when they admit they have a problem. But leave when it is necessary.

Five days later amidst the struggles and uncertainties we faced, Kenny reached out to me with a heartfelt offer—he wanted to bring me dinner. It was a small gesture, but it held significant meaning for both of us. Table talk over a meal is where we always came to understand the trials we faced. As he arrived with the meal, we found ourselves drawn to prayer, seeking guidance from our heavenly Father. He looked in my eyes many times as if he was looking straight through my soul. This was also indicative of the fact that at this moment he wasn't hiding the pupils of someone under the influence.

In an intimate moment, he touched my face and expressed a deep realization—he acknowledged that he had reached a point in his life where he could no longer afford to relapse. He recognized the toll it had taken on him, me, and Nathaniel and the importance of committing to a life of sobriety. With conviction in his voice, he promised that he would never use drugs again. I kissed him goodnight and watched as he drove away.

That night became a pivotal moment, a turning point marked by a profound sense of gratitude and hope. However, the challenges persisted, and my heart remained entwined with Kenny's journey. Little did I know that just a few days later, our paths would intersect in the most devastating way imaginable.

On July 3rd, I received a life-altering phone call from the hospital. The news pierced through my soul: Mrs. LaTampa, your husband is on life-support, and you are urgently needed to make critical decisions about his care. The shock and anguish flooded over me. Through tears I quickly made phone calls to Kenny's mother, my mother, and my best friend Jenn, notifying them of the situation. With a sense of urgency, I rushed to the hospital, the weight of the moment heavy on my heart. I know I must have run red lights. In those mere five minutes it took me to get to the hospital, a whirlwind of emotions coursed through me.

Upon arrival, I was met with the stark reality that due to COVID concerns, I would be the only one allowed to enter the hospital. The thought of being separated from loved ones during such a critical time was a heavy burden to bear. Nevertheless, I gathered my strength and resolve, understanding that I needed to be there for Kenny.

As I made my way inside, a masked nurse approached me with a gentle presence. Later I would find out that it was actually someone I knew from high school. She offered a glimmer of hope, asking if I would like to speak to Kenny. In that moment, my heart swelled with excitement, hoping for a chance to connect with him, to offer words of love and encouragement.

However, her words shattered my anticipation as she shared that the purpose of the conversation would be to say goodbye. The reality of the situation crashed over me like a tidal wave, overwhelming me with grief and disbelief. It was an unimaginable blow, a moment that would forever be etched in my memory.

Upon speaking with the doctor and receiving the devastating news that Kenny had suffered an overdose and then an anoxic brain injury, the weight of the situation became all too real. The gravity of the situation settled heavily upon me, and I knew I had to make the difficult decision that no one should ever have to face.

Despite the shock and pain, I gathered my composure, realizing that this would be the last opportunity to express my love, to offer words of comfort and reassurance to Kenny. With a heavy heart, I entered the room, steeling myself for the emotional journey that lay ahead.

In that sacred space, surrounded by the hum of medical equipment, I muttered, "I love you, Kenny. You said you were done; this was not what was supposed to happen." I had gone to war in prayer for him many times in the spirit but all I could muster up through the tears was the Lord's Prayer.

Our Father, who art in heaven,

Hallowed be thy Name.

Thy Kingdom come,

Thy will be done,

On earth as it is in heaven.

Give us this day our daily bread.

And forgive us our trespasses,

As we forgive those who trespass against us.

And lead us not into temptation,

But deliver us from evil.

Amen.

I touched his face, the faint smell of his body wash lingering in the air. I could not hold back tears as I spoke in words of love, gratitude, and the hope of eternal peace. Hunny, if you can hear me, if there is anything you need to repent of, please do so now. I assured him that he was not alone, and that God's presence would guide him on his next journey.

Through tears and trembling words, I held onto the promise of a life beyond this earthly realm, where pain and suffering would be no more. I prayed in my head for Kenny's peace, for his soul to find rest in the arms of our Heavenly Father.

As I said my final goodbyes, a profound mix of emotions washed over me—grief, loss, but also a sense of hope and trust in God's ultimate plan. I knew that this moment, as heart-wrenching as it was, was not the end. Kenny's spirit would live on, and our connection would endure in the memories we had created and the love we shared.

With a heavy heart, I made the phone call to Kenny's mother, and together, we embarked on the painful journey of making a decision regarding his medical care. In the face of this profound and irreversible injury, we confronted the reality that continuing measures would only prolong his suffering.

It was a heart-wrenching choice, filled with sorrow and anguish. We knew that this decision would forever alter the course of our lives, but we also understood that it was a compassionate act, allowing Kenny to find peace and release from his pain.

In the depths of our grief, we shared our love for Kenny and our desire to honor his well-being.

As we made the decision to cease measures, we held on to the hope that Kenny would find comfort in the arms of our heavenly Father. We knew that his spirit would be free from the confines of his earthly body, liberated from the pain and limitations that he had endured.

When Kenny's mother and stepfather arrived at the hospital, I knew that it was essential for them to have private time with him, to say their final goodbyes. In a moment of strength and understanding, I quietly walked down the corridor and made my way towards the exit front doors.

There, waiting for me outside, were my best friend and her husband, understanding and supportive through every step of this agonizing journey. As I saw their familiar faces, the weight of the situation crashed down upon me, and I couldn't contain the overwhelming surge of emotions any longer. A guttural scream escaped from deep within me, an outpouring of grief, pain, and unimaginable loss.

At that moment, my knees became weak, and my best friend and her husband held me in their arms, providing a safe space for my anguish.

They held me as I let my grief flow freely, offering a shoulder to lean on, and providing unwavering support in the face of immense sorrow.

Together, we stood there, allowing the depth of my pain to be felt and acknowledged. In their presence, I found strength, comfort, and the assurance that I was not alone in this heartbreaking moment.

Their loving embrace and understanding presence became a lifeline, grounding me in the midst of the storm. Their unwavering presence became a testament to the power of friendship and love. It was in that moment, amidst the rawness of my pain, that I realized the profound impact of their support. They had been there for me through the birth of my son, my divorce, my miscarriages, and Kenny's relapses. Their support sustained me through many life events, and it would continue through the days, weeks, months, and years ahead.

As the sobs subsided and the tears continued to flow, my best friend and her husband remained by my side, offering a comforting presence and an unwavering commitment to walk with me through the journey of grief and healing.

After collecting myself, I gathered the strength to enter back into the hospital alone and into the ICU room again, where his mother and stepfather stood, his mother tenderly holding his hand and pushing his hair away from his brow. I asked her if she had told him it was ok to go. She nodded and again spoke to him of our shared belief that it was alright for him to join Jesus in the afterlife.

In that very moment, he peacefully transitioned from this life to eternal glory, leaving us with the memory of his presence and the reassurance that he was now in a better place and holding the baby we had lost.

Superman's Demise

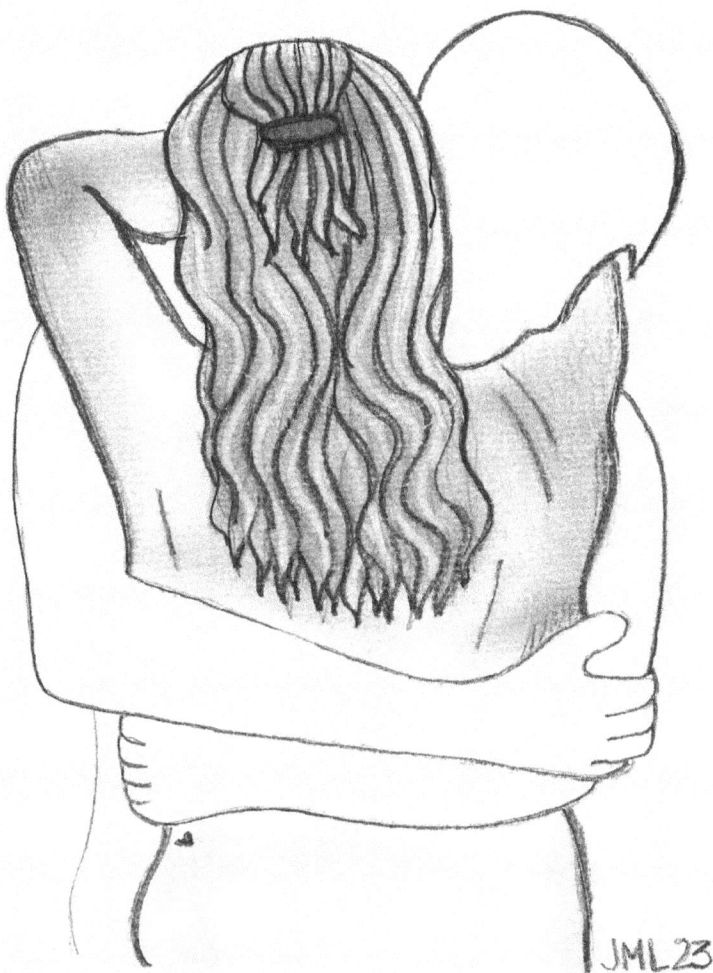

Grief

Psalm 56:8

You have taken account of my wanderings; Put my tears in Your bottle. Are they not in Your book?

And so my grief began. My best friend drove me home and that morning, we leaned on one another, finding peace and compassion in shared memories, stories, and the love that bound us all together. She and her husband have become my pillars of strength, providing a source of stability and a reminder that, even in the depths of despair, there is hope to be found in the bonds of friendship.

In the days that followed, my best friend and her husband continued to be a constant source of support, offering a listening ear, a compassionate heart, and a presence that reminded me I was never alone. They walked with me through the stages of grief, reminded me to eat, and helped me navigate the complexities of loss and find brief moments of healing and renewal.

Though the pain of losing Kenny would forever remain, the support of my best friend and her husband became a source of inspiration and helped me find the strength to face each day and my new reality.

I am forever grateful for their friendship, for the way they held space for my grief, and for reminding me that, even in the midst of unimaginable loss, love and connection can offer reassurance. I hold on to all they provided, cherishing the memory of them, carrying friendship with me as a precious gift.

During those first few weeks I found myself constantly praying. But in the depths of my grief, I questioned God about why He didn't answer my prayers and heal my husband's drug addiction. I struggled to understand why my heartfelt pleas seemingly went unanswered. However, as I navigated through the pain and sorrow, I eventually found comfort in a different perspective. I came to realize that God did, in fact, answer my prayers, but in a way that I couldn't initially comprehend. He granted my husband total healing by freeing him from the chains of addiction through his passing. Though it was a difficult truth to accept, I found reassurance in knowing that my husband was finally at peace and completely healed in God's embrace.

Jenn often reminded me that Kenny's work here was done. Even with that understanding the days that followed were filled with a mix of grief, remembrance, and a deep sense of loss. From writing my husband's obituary, to assisting in carrying his casket, picking up his ashes, the medical examiner's findings, moving all of his belongings to my small apartment and realizing that the man he saw so much potential in was the one who gave him the drugs that would end his life.

I felt guilty and ashamed. The weeks after Kenny's death were a huge struggle. I forced myself to get up and go to church, I forced myself to go to work, I forced myself to shower, I forced myself to sleep, I read our messages over and over wondering if I missed something, I forced myself to stop reading his journals. There were days that I cried in front of family, fellow workers, the church, strangers, and my son. The tears would overwhelm me at times over what seemed silly. Seeing his favorite donuts at the grocery store, memories on my social media, a song playing on the radio. But I continued to go back to the last message he sent me. It said:

Take heart.

He bottles your tears for a reason.

I just want you to understand what I know. I love you more than you think.

Questions always swirled in my mind. It consumed me. Did I love him enough? Did my leaving cause his death? Sometimes your anger fuels your strength. Your loss becomes a passion. You find a voice you never knew existed. Your soul comes alive using your grief as a tool. Your pain pushes you toward a path that becomes your new purpose.

At times I would feel a little reassurance. People would encourage me and say your journey is now to honor your husband, to educate the public about this misunderstood disease. To prevent another person's overdose or heartbreak.

People would say, "You received an education you didn't sign up for. You are now addiction's widow… You loved and lost your husband. You are his voice. You are his warrior."

All I thought was, "Yes his fight is over. But do you realize mine has just begun?"

There were days I did feel like a warrior. I would tell myself, "You were the wife of an addict. You will not be silenced. In you he will live on forever." Then my mind would go back to, God is there something I could have done differently? These are things that were constantly tormenting me. But a friend of mine continually reminded me that the Thursday before the night he died we had spent the evening together. An evening filled with honesty.

She was right. I was honest. He had asked me to leave, but I had also left because that was the only way I knew how to love him. He had brought me dinner. Prayed before our meal. He rubbed my legs and told me that I needed to take care of myself. He asked if I felt safe. He said that I should get double locks on the doors. He assured me that he would continue to pay bills, because he was still my husband and that was his responsibility.

One afternoon I sat weeping. I was going through all of his receipts. He always worked so hard. I happened upon the last pile crying with tears that overcame me. In that last pile was a local lumber store gift card. To my surprise it still had $88 on it. Just another sign that the Lord and my husband would continue to provide for me.

I continue to rehash events that pricked my heart. At the calling hours, someone told Nathaniel in a private conversation, "At least your real dad isn't dead." It shattered his heart and mine. The remarkable bond shared between Kenny and Nathaniel was undeniable, transcending the confines of a biological connection. Kenny might not have been Nathaniel's biological father, and he may not have always got things right, but he was undeniably a father figure who played an essential role in his life.

Their extraordinary relationship highlighted the truth that fatherhood goes beyond mere genetics, finding its roots in love, care, and shared experiences. The callous comment only served as a reminder of the profound loss Nathaniel felt and the love he held for Kenny, whose influence as a father figure remained ever-present, even in his absence.

It's unfortunate that during sensitive times like Kenny's calling hours, people sometimes say thoughtless things without intending to be cruel. People might not fully understand the impact of their words or may struggle to find the right words to offer comfort. I tried to remember, everyone copes differently, and it's important to be patient and forgiving, even when hurtful comments are made.

It's often a lack of awareness rather than intentional cruelty. I myself also had disheartened comments from others that to this day sting. In the midst of my grief people told me he wasn't in heaven, that by choosing drugs and overdosing he had taken his own life. I found myself seeking God and the scriptures in my grief. Why would anyone make comments like that to a grieving wife and son?

I found peace in what the Bible actually says about those who believe in Jesus but continue to walk in addiction. While the Bible doesn't specifically address drug overdoses, it does offer general principles about God's character and forgiveness. One commonly cited verse is Romans 8:38-39, which says, "For I am convinced that neither death nor life, neither angels nor demons, neither the present nor the future, nor any powers, neither height nor depth, nor anything else in all creation, will be able to separate us from the love of God that is in Christ Jesus our Lord." This verse was a reminder of God's unwavering love and grace, regardless of circumstances.

"And know that I am with you always; yes, to the end of time."—Matthew 28:20. Jesus doesn't say "unless you are an addict." He does not have conditions. No matter how much someone may have distanced themselves from Jesus or how badly their addiction becomes, Jesus will be with them so long as they accept him.

"Come to me, all who labor and are heavy laden, and I will give you rest."—Matthew 11:28. Jesus asks us to come to him with our anxieties and our problems. No matter what these problems are, addiction included, if we trust in him, he will give us hope. With hope, we can find peace even at our death.

Even amidst his struggles with addiction, there were unmistakable signs that Kenny's love for Jesus remained unwavering. His conversations often centered around his faith, and his eyes lit up when discussing spiritual matters. Despite the darkness that addiction brought, his heart remained open to God's love and forgiveness. He would share verses from the Bible that resonated with him, and his prayers and petitions were always very sincere and heartfelt. Even in his lowest moments, you could see the spark of hope and faith flickering within him, a testament to his connection to Jesus.

As I read Kenny's journals the first week after his death I realized the man who went to the streets and prayed for other addicts and the homeless struggled on a daily basis. It broke my heart that I didn't see this while he was alive. His struggles, his insecurities, were always covered. I always called him Superman for a reason. He portrayed that on the outside. But on the inside, I realized he was full of sorrow, grief that included childhood trauma.

Reading through my husband's journals, I discovered his heartfelt pleas to be freed from the clutches of addiction. His words revealed his deep yearning for God's intervention, hoping to break free from the chains that held him captive. It was full of questions. Why can't I overcome it? Why do I hurt the ones that love me?

In those pages, I found his raw vulnerability as he laid bare his pain and regrets. He didn't just seek salvation for himself; he also prayed for me and my son, Nathaniel, praying for our healing from the anguish his addiction caused. It's evident that he cared deeply for both of us and wanted to mend the bonds that his struggles had strained.

My conviction that he's now in heaven speaks to my strong faith and the love we shared. Despite the tragic circumstances that led to his passing, I hold on to the belief that he's found peace beyond his earthly struggles. My journey through his journals offered insight into his innermost thoughts, and it's a testament to the complex and profound nature of his love for Jesus.

My emotions continued to be everywhere, when I began to journal myself.

This is a short excerpt from my journal, July 30, 2020

I want my life back.

I want it the way it used to be when things were good.

I want to sit in the front seat of his truck, Nathaniel sitting in the back, wind in my hair, his hand in mine, sun shining on my face, no destination, just his loud music and quick glances.

I want to get a phone call or text message telling me Good Morning or asking when I would be coming home.

I want to watch him trim his walrus mustache.

I want someone else to help make decisions.

I want someone to be standing there when I am praying with someone.

I want to share my revelations, or my good news or for that matter even the bad.

I want to discuss where we are going to eat to just end up going to his favorite place "Olive Garden."

I want to make a pot of coffee, not just a single cup.

I want to lay beside him, head on his chest and arm around his waist.

I want to look across the room and see him

Playing scatter slots. (I was so jealous of that game.)

I want to sit In the bathroom and discuss our day as he showered after work.

I want him to yell upstairs, "Jo, are you ready yet?

I want morning prayers.

I want his soft kiss on my neck as I wash the dishes.

I want to hear his laugh and I love you's.

I want to hear him say how good his clothes smell after I have washed them.

I want to hear him say, "You look cute today."

I want him to rub my legs after a long day at work.

I want to hear him say, "Did you turn the heat down again?"

I want to chuckle at his inability to clap his hands and sing at the same time.

No, I don't want arguments.

No, I don't want the worries of another relapse.

No, I don't want the codependency back.

No, I don't want the pain.

I don't want to cry anymore.

I don't want to see the pain in my son's eyes.

No, I definitely don't want to wait to see him again.

But hey, we don't always get what we want in this life do we?

....

"The Lord directs our steps, so why try to understand everything along the way?"

It brought tears to my eyes as I reread it. As I tried to put my feelings into words, it's almost overwhelming to think about the mix of emotions that had consumed me. The grief was heavy, and along with it, there was for a short time a burning anger that I couldn't shake off.

I found myself asking, "Why did he pick up drugs again after promising not to?" The broken promises cut deep, and I couldn't help but wonder if he truly loved me. Did his actions mean he chose drugs over his own life, over our life together? It was a turmoil of thoughts and feelings that kept replaying in my mind.

I know that addiction is a powerful and complex force, but it's so hard to reconcile the person I loved with the choices he made. The anger simmered beneath the surface, and at times, it felt like it was consuming me. I tried to remind myself that love and addiction are not always mutually exclusive, but it's difficult not to feel betrayed.

Navigating through the anger amidst my grief proved to be a challenging uphill journey. While I wished to pay tribute to his memory and the cherished moments we shared, the anger I felt seemed to stand as an insurmountable obstacle. The path through grief was intricate and multifaceted, requiring me to approach it with patience, taking each day as it came. Surprisingly, as time went on, the anger gradually receded, allowing me to remember him with fondness and warmth.

I want to share something important. I've come to realize that he didn't choose drugs over me. He didn't choose drugs over his family or his friends and he definitely didn't choose to die. His struggle with addiction was incredibly difficult, and I believe that the weight of those challenges eventually overwhelmed him. I've come to understand that addiction is a complex battle, and it's not just a matter of making choices. He fought his own demons, and despite my and others presence and support, those struggles became too much for him to bear.

In moments of reflection, I've felt God's grace, particularly when contemplating Kenny's overdose. It crossed my mind that perhaps God allowed this tragedy as a form of mercy, liberating him from the relentless demons of addiction, pain, and inner struggles. This perspective also extended mercy to me and many others, alleviating the burden of worry and fear we carried almost daily. Maybe God protected all of us in ways unseen. While the pain remains, these thoughts offer peace in the belief that God's grace works in ways we may not fully comprehend.

After enduring most of my husband's relapses, I found myself repeatedly losing valuable possessions that held deep sentimental meaning. However, this particular time was different. Kenny had left behind many tools and work equipment. It was an unexpected gift amidst the difficulties. What touched my heart even more was the unwavering dedication of my father. He labored tirelessly, putting in tremendous effort to sell Kenny's tools and equipment. This endeavor was difficult for me, letting go of Kenny's possessions he had worked so hard for. I know God was ensuring my survival financially in the midst of this turmoil. My father's selflessness and hard work provided me with the financial stability I needed in the upcoming months. In moments of struggle, I also received the reports of that night from the local police department. I found that although the man who supplied him drugs could have left my husband after his overdose, he had called 911. I am grateful for this action. I am not sure of the trauma it would have caused if I had been the one who found him days later.

The sweet-spirited nurse contacted me because she was an acquaintance of ours in school. She spoke of knowing how much I loved Kenny, that when the paramedics arrived in her ER department, they had said a family member had called 911. The hospital assumed that person was me. She continued to ask doctors to reach out to me knowing that if I was the one who had called, I would have been there at my husband's bedside, and I was not. Her persistence led to that fateful phone call. Without her Kenny would have passed alone, and I and his parents would not have had our closure with our goodbyes.

My father, son, and best friend held vigil over me for the months that followed and navigated me through the waves of grief. I had the presence of family, friends, and our faith community. I leaned on God's promises, trusting that He would bring healing to my broken heart and grant me the strength to carry on. I held on to the belief that Kenny's spirit lived on, forever a part of our lives and forever held in the embrace of God's love.

Through the pain and the continuing dull ache, I find comfort in the hope of a future reunion, where I will be united with Kenny, my baby, and so many more I cherish in a place where suffering and separation are no more.

Grief can destroy you—or focus you. You can decide a relationship was all for nothing if it had to end in death, and you're alone or you can realize that every moment of it had more meaning than you dared to recognize at the time, so much meaning it scared you, so you just lived, just took for granted the love and laughter of each day and didn't allow yourself to consider the sacredness of it.

When it's over and you're crying alone, you begin to see that it wasn't just having a companion. He was my living journal—he knew all my secrets. The way he loved that chair we got off a trash route, the way he debated with Nathaniel, the way he fought for a rescued bird's attention and after many bloody bites she relented, or the way he prayed with strangers, or the vacations, or the memories as I pass the houses daily that he did repairs on, or the midnight calls to get someone into rehab, his horrible snoring, watching the clouds and rain together, him calling me stubborn and telling me to get over it or listening to music with prophetic ears, or worrying over a high electric bill, or lying in bed till three in the morning talking about the deeper things of God, or the fact that during the day we were so connected we would be eating the same thing but twenty miles away in different locations, or driving down the road to see his tattooed arm wave at me because we were traveling in the same area for work, the way he smelled, and the way when we argued his charm and smile would make my heart sink. The way he could manipulate any situation when he called me sugar, the way we discussed our dreams, the way we delved into each symbolism biblically, the photos he secretly had taken that I found on his phone, one's of me washing dishes or sleeping, his half Woody Woodpecker laugh, his forgiving heart, his Godfidence, his Superman hair swoop, his knowledge and wisdom on so many levels, or the gift that arrived on our anniversary after his death, which happened to be a fork and spoon with hearts on them, a God wink symbolizing to me he would be attending the great marriage supper, but mostly his walk in Christ.

Kenny and I shared a bond that some might describe as peculiar. We had a unique understanding of each other, often finding humor and solace in the most unusual ideas and revelations. One such notion was our playful teasing about what might happen if one of us were to pass away before the other. Kenny would often say I'm asking God for my own solar system. Oddly enough the night he passed there was a solar eclipse. We whimsically mused frequently that we would petition God to grant us the extraordinary privilege of entering each other's dreams to share the revelation of heaven. It was a lighthearted and imaginative notion, born out of our deep friendship and our love for dream interpretations and also, I suppose the desire to remain connected even in the face of mortality.

While there may not be a specific scriptural reference to such dreams, the Bible does acknowledge the significance of dreams as a means of communication and revelation. In Acts 2:17, the apostle Peter quotes the prophet Joel, proclaiming, "In the last days, God says, I will pour out my Spirit on all people. Your sons and daughters will prophesy, your young men will see visions, your old men will dream dreams." This verse highlights the idea that dreams can carry spiritual meaning and may be a conduit through which God communicates with us.

Though our playful fantasy may not align precisely with scriptural teachings, it still brings immense peace to my heart. Even after Kenny's passing, I find myself dreaming of him, and in those reveries, he appears whole and healed, radiating a sense of peace and joy with his smile that carries so much charm that surpasses all earthly understanding. While I may not fully comprehend the divine nature of these dreams, they serve as a constant reminder of the profound connection we shared in life. They allow me to cherish his memory and find comfort in the belief that he is in a place of eternal serenity.

As I continue to dream of Kenny, it's as if a thread of our relationship lingers on, transcending the boundaries of time and space. Our shared jest about God's involvement in our dreams remains a cherished part of our story, a testament to the enduring power of friendship and love. In these dreams, I glimpse the essence of who Kenny truly was—a kind, compassionate soul with an infectious spirit. Smiling at me with the charm he carried. While our earthly journey together may have come to an end, the memories we created and the dreams that follow keep his presence alive in my heart.

And so, I find comfort in the thought that even in the vastness of heaven, our bond endures, bringing me peace, joy, and a glimmer of hope for what lies beyond this life.

It was never perfect, there was arguing, periods of silence and withdrawal, there was heartache and tears, there was huge lapses of judgements on both our parts and for me there is still much regret. But it was my everything, it was the why of my life, every event and precious moment of it. The answer to the mystery of existence is the love we shared sometimes so imperfectly, and when the loss wakes you to the deeper beauty of it, to the sanctity of it, you can't get off your knees for long. You're driven to your knees not by the weight of the loss but by gratitude for what preceded the loss.

And the ache is always there, but maybe one day not the emptiness, because to nurture the emptiness, to take solace in it, is to disrespect the gift of the life I shared with him. It is truly better to have loved and lost, than to never have loved at all. Nathaniel during my grief stated, "Mom, we should not be sad he is gone. We should be happy that we enjoyed him for a season." I added some of these quotes that truly assisted me in understanding grief. Although all are unique, they are also relatable.

"Grief is the last act of love we have to give to those we loved. Where there is deep grief, there is great love." - Unknown

"The darker the night, the brighter the stars, The deeper the grief, the closer is God!" - Fyodor Dostoevsky

"Grief, no matter how you try to cater to its wail, has a way of fading away." - V.C. Andrews

"When someone you love becomes a memory, the memory becomes a treasure." - Unknown

"The reality is that you will grieve forever. You will not 'get over' the loss of a loved one; you will learn to live with it. You will heal and you will rebuild yourself around the loss you have suffered. You will be whole again, but you will never be the same. Nor should you be the same, nor would you want to." - Elisabeth Kubler-Ross

"Tears shed for another person are not a sign of weakness. They are a sign of a pure heart." - José N. Harris

"What we have once enjoyed deeply, we can never lose. All that we love deeply becomes a part of us." - Helen Keller

One of the things I have discovered is that the presence of grief fills up a lot of the space that the affection and love for my husband once occupied, and letting go of that pain, in a strange way, feels like I'm letting go of him. I understand why we choose to hold on to that sorrow because it's holding on to a person. There were many times I wished I was determined enough to push it away.

Half of my conversations still involve some aspect of him. What he would say, what he would do. I heard a quote today: "Do you not know that a man is not dead while his name is still spoken?" I think there is a lot of truth behind this quote.

Over the years I tried to talk to other men and have been asked to dinner. Although Kenny and I had many trials, there was always a comparison. Maybe I was critical, maybe I was not ready, maybe I didn't give people a chance. It always brings me back to this emotional rewind thinking about his charm, his love for Jesus, and those hurting, and it spirals down to the call from the hospital, or the last night we spent together, watching him drive away, not knowing I would never hear his voice again, I would never kiss him again, I would never argue with him again, and I felt like I would never move forward.

But as grief unfolded, at times a peculiar sensation settled in, almost as if the story were embracing the contours of a fairytale ending or conclusion.

In the midst of this juncture, I shared one final night with my husband before his passing. Amidst remembering the bittersweet moments, it was as if a narrative had tied up loose ends with a graceful bow.

I guess It's not about pushing yourself through being miserable. I understand the feeling of frustrated impatience, when you just pray that things could be better already, when you know that this is dragging out and you just want to feel better.

There's a reason everyone says that everyone grieves differently—they do. Some people take years and years to recover from things that other people might emotionally process in months or even weeks.

You feel like you're overcoming and then, even like today you wake-up, and for a moment, everything is calm. Then, in a rush, it all comes flooding back; you remember what you've lost. Your throat closes, your stomach heaves. You didn't think you had any tears left to cry, but now they're streaming down your cheeks like a waterfall. Your chest is tight, and it feels hard to breathe. You don't know how you will face the day ahead, and you feel alone in your pain.

People mistakenly believe that "grief" is a single emotion, but it is actually a complex, multifaceted response to loss. Others may not see it, but you learn to live with the pain through the weeks and months to accommodate your new reality. However, the true tragedy of the loss tends to unfold in layers over time again and again.

We don't talk enough about grieving and its onslaught of confused emotions. One moment you want to cry and the next you want to laugh. One moment you feel relief and the next you feel guilt...for feeling relief.

But my grief does not define me. I know that you can both grieve and laugh; that you can miss someone with your entire body and want to love another with that same body; that you can mourn a loss while looking into a future filled with hope and promise but honestly, it's the good memories that hurt the most.

There is nothing in my life right now that's perfect. This isn't working out the way anybody thought it would. So I guess it's ok that I still cry, I'm still sad, I still wish so many things had gone differently—but truth be told I wouldn't undo any of this if I could.

Transformation is good, the process is not always welcoming, but I know God has a plan for my future and just like anyone else I will continue to overcome.

In times of grief, pain becomes an undeniable companion. It's an intensely emotional experience that can leave us feeling overwhelmed and vulnerable. The pain of loss can manifest in various ways—from an aching emptiness in our hearts to a profound sense of sadness that seems to linger. It's important to recognize that experiencing pain is a natural response to losing someone we love deeply.

When we encounter such profound pain, Jesus' teachings can be a source of solace and healing. In the Bible, Jesus himself experienced deep sorrow and grief, allowing us to find comfort in knowing that He understands our pain. He offers empathy and compassion, reminding us that we are not alone in our suffering.

During these difficult moments, a loved one's support takes on an even more significant role. They can be a comforting presence, offering a listening ear and a shoulder to lean on.

The love and understanding shared among family members can provide a safe space to express our pain openly and honestly, allowing us to process our emotions and begin the journey towards healing.

In addition to seeking support from friends and family, turning to our faith in Jesus can help us find strength in the midst of pain. Through prayer and reflection on His teachings, we may discover a sense of peace and hope. Jesus' promise of eternal life and His message of love can bring comfort and reassurance that our loved ones are not truly lost but waiting for us in a better place.

As we navigate the path of grief, it's essential to be gentle with ourselves and give ourselves the time and space needed to heal. The pain may not fully dissipate, but with the support of Jesus, family, and our faith, we can find the resilience to move forward, carrying the cherished memories of our loved ones in our hearts forever.

In the midst of overwhelming grief, my heart aches, and my eyes leak as I dearly miss Kenny. He was my best friend and husband. However, amid the pain, I find solace in the comforting belief that he will be there to greet me as I enter heaven. Our eternal connection and cherished memories bring hope and strength as I navigate through the healing process. Though the void left by his absence is profound, the thought of our eventual reunion fills me with love and joy. Until that day comes, I will hold on to our precious bond, knowing that our love will endure beyond this lifetime. I find comfort in the fact that Kenny understood my deepest emotions and our shared peculiarities, making him not just my Superman but also my kryptonite. His presence lifted me to great heights, but paradoxically, losing him became my own vulnerability. Despite the pain, I draw inspiration from his superhero-like qualities to find resilience during this difficult journey. And while the void he left can never be filled, the belief that he will meet me at the gates of heaven someday brings peace and hope to my heart. Until that moment arrives, I will cherish his memory, guided by the certainty of our eternal connection and the everlasting love we hold for each other.

The truth is that we never get over the people we lose but it's understandable that finding ways to move forward in our lives and be in the world without the people we love can feel daunting when you are going through a big loss.

Through my grief I overcame so many varying emotions, such as anger, disappointment, envy, self-doubt, sadness, guilt, and anxiety that have brought me to my knees. It has never crippled me, but it is definitely hard to navigate all of those feelings I listed, especially when you feel different ones day to day, or even hour to hour. Writing about what I'm feeling is one of the best ways to move through the roller coaster of emotions, but it also allows me to go back and see how far I have come.

When you break your arm, no one ever says, "Hey, get over it. Go back to what you were doing the day before it happened. Hurry up. Heal, that doesn't hurt!" Oftentimes there is a cast there to remind everyone of your injury. They rally around you; they help you carry the things that are too heavy.

But when it comes to grief, you can't see the pain and after a week or two people stop calling, people stop dropping by, texting, and reaching out. Physical wounds normally don't heal overnight; the healing process almost always requires time—possibly weeks or months or maybe even years. Similarly, a deep emotional or mental wound won't normally heal fully from a quick-fix solution. Grief especially requires time and help from others who care about us.

Grief doesn't magically end at a certain point after a loved one's death. Reminders often bring back the pain of loss.

Certain reminders of your loved one might be inevitable, such as the anniversary of the person's death, holidays, birthdays, or new events you know he or she would have enjoyed. (Or in my case all of them in the same month…July.) Even memorial celebrations for others can trigger the pain of your own loss.

God is good, but sometimes healing comes slowly. Rapid healing might not bring you to persistently cast your burdens on God in the same way a slow healing process would.

More than that, we rejoice in our sufferings, knowing that suffering produces endurance, and endurance produces character, and character produces hope, and hope does not put us to shame, because God's love has been poured into our hearts through the Holy Spirit who has been given to us.

When healing goes very slowly, or even ceases at some point, we have the opportunity to testify that our strength doesn't come from within but rather from the power of Christ in us. Suffering also helps us not to hold on too tightly to the things of this world and to remember that we belong to God.

Take heart if you're grieving that one day you will have complete healing—physically, emotionally, and spiritually—and are at this very moment a co-heir with Christ. No one can snatch you out of Jesus' loving hand, and you are safe and secure in Christ forevermore.

Grief

A Pandemic

Revelation 2:11

"He who has an ear, let him hear what the Spirit says to the churches. He who overcomes shall not be hurt by the second death."

Widowhood. I still cringe when I hear the word. It's not what I would have chosen, and it's certainly not what I expected for this time in my life. Widowhood is carrying heartbreak alone and realizing no one can share that pain with you as he could.

For most couples out there, when you stand in front of the person you have chosen to do life with, promising "till death do we part," you don't think about the day you will inevitably part. I know I didn't.

No, widowhood at forty-five was not what I expected. I've learned what it is. It's coming home at the end of a tough day of work to an empty house, no one to sit at the table with at dinner, longing to have my husband's strong arms wrap around me as I allow the cares of the world to melt away in his embrace.

It's planning for the future without having someone to plan with. Someone who is equally invested in your hopes and dreams to hope and dream with. Someday, after retirement, we were going to get a Winnebago, fill it with Bibles to hand out and travel to the west coast. Now there's no more talk of someday and retirement. Now retirement is something I dread rather than anticipate.

It's going out to eat and hearing the hostess say, "Just one?" Then hearing her words echo throughout dinner as you gaze at the elderly couple sitting across from you at the next table, carried away in endless chatter as you sit in solitude.

For the first year I had so much regret. So much guilt. Even some resentment. Selfish thoughts that Kenny was gone, and he left me to deal with all of this life all alone. How unfair! There were dark times when I even thought how much easier he had it. How ridiculous, right?

Much of the anger and numbness as I stated quickly began to get replaced with acceptance and fortitude. Sadness was still there.

Experiencing the tangible love of God amid the challenging circumstances of COVID was yet another profound and transformative journey.

The media played a crucial role in disseminating information about COVID-19. While many outlets focused on accurate reporting and public health guidance, there were instances where sensationalism took center stage. Some media coverage highlighted worst-case scenarios, which contributed to fear and anxiety among the public.

This fear was often fueled by constant updates, dramatic imagery, and attention-grabbing headlines. As a result, people became more anxious about the virus's potential impact, leading to panic buying, misinformation, and an overall sense of uncertainty. The media's portrayal of COVID-19 showcased a complex balance between informing the public and unintentionally amplifying fear and hysteria.

Working in healthcare we were required to test weekly. Four months after Kenny's passing, I was one of the first to test positive and contract COVID amongst my friends, family, and colleagues.

At first fear and uncertainty gripped me, but I soon realized that there was a divine presence guiding me through the ordeal. Though I didn't suffer from severe symptoms, I did struggle with a persistent and debilitating headache for three days. Unable to retest and get access to return to work. I was then isolated from peers for an arduous fifty-seven days. With no income during this period and unable to return to work without a negative test, the situation felt overwhelming.

During the pandemic, the already challenging journey of being a widow became even more difficult for me. Dealing with the profound loss of my spouse was a heavy burden to bear, and the pandemic added another layer of complexity to my grieving process. The inability to qualify for pandemic relief created financial strain, further intensifying the stress I was experiencing. The social isolation and restrictions that came with the pandemic made it even harder to cope with my grief, as I felt disconnected from my usual support network.

The changes in routines and daily life that the pandemic brought about forced me to confront new challenges on a regular basis. The uncertainty and constant adjustments only added to the overwhelming sense of vulnerability and sadness that I was already grappling with. As the world around me seemed to transform, I found myself struggling to find stability and a sense of normalcy amidst the chaos.

Throughout this difficult period, finding ways to adapt and seek solace became paramount. Virtual connections with friends and family became a lifeline, offering moments of comfort and a way to share my emotions.

The journey through grief is never easy, and the pandemic undoubtedly added unprecedented challenges to an already painful experience. But through resilience, adaptability, and seeking God, I found ways to cope and gradually make my way through this added trial.

We are all too familiar with the days it all just feels like too much. We know it can be difficult to see the promises of God through the things we are experiencing. We start to feel alone in what we're facing. I remember reading this scripture as I sat at my kitchen table alone.

Lamentations 3:22-23: "The steadfast love of the LORD never ceases; His mercies never come to an end; they are new every morning; great is Your faithfulness."

His mercies never come to an end. Every morning, even the ones filled with anxieties and what ifs and sorrow, He gives us new mercies.

I tried my best to cope with these new adversities. Seeking support from friends, family, and even virtual communities was crucial in finding some comfort. Though it wasn't easy, I took one step at a time. It was during this time of isolation that I truly experienced the depth of God's love and care. I found comfort in prayer and a renewed connection with my faith. Each day, I sought strength and hope from a higher power, and in return, I felt a sense of peace that transcended my circumstances.

During my period of isolation, I stumbled upon a remarkable discovery. The surplus of time that isolation granted me turned out to be a gift, enabling me to engage in activities that I had previously only dabbled in. One of the most significant changes was my newfound dedication to intercede for the health concerns of my immunocompromised loved ones.

With the world slowing down and external distractions fading away, I found myself drawn to a place of deep reflection. As I contemplated the fragility of health and the uncertainty that often accompanies it, I realized the power of intention and positive energy. So, I began to weave heartfelt prayers and thoughts for my loved ones into my daily routine, fervently hoping for their improved well-being.

This practice of intercession transformed into an emotional anchor, a way for me to feel connected and involved even while physically apart. As each day unfolded, I could sense a sense of purpose building within me—a purpose driven by love and concern for those I held dear. It was a silver lining amidst the challenging times, an unexpected avenue for meaningful engagement and support.

But there was more. Amidst the quietude of isolation, I turned to the blank pages of my sketchbook. Drawing, an art form I had once merely dabbled in, became a refuge for my thoughts and emotions. The strokes of graphite or ink on paper were a way to translate the complex tapestry of feelings swirling within me into tangible imagery. Every stroke, every detail added, was a step towards externalizing the intricate web of emotions that isolation had woven around me.

Each drawing became a story, a visual representation of a moment, a feeling, or a hope. It wasn't just about the final outcome but the process itself—the gradual manifestation of an idea, the patience required to bring it to life, and the catharsis that accompanied the entire artistic journey.

In the grand scheme of my isolation experience, these two practices— intercession for my loved ones' health and the newfound devotion to drawing—stood out. They provided me with purpose, a sense of connection, and a channel for creative expression that I had never fully embraced before. While isolation brought its own challenges, it also presented me with opportunities for personal growth, deep introspection, and a new way to connect with both my inner self and the world around me.

Amid the trying days of isolation, the unwavering support and love from my family and friends shone as a beacon of hope. Unable to visit in person due to safety concerns, they found creative ways to show their care and concern. They regularly brought me delicious homemade meals and surprise gifts, left at my doorstep like tokens of love. Each meal felt like a warm hug, and every gift brought a smile to my face, reminding me of the thoughtful presence my family and friends had in my life.

Their gestures were more than just food and gifts; they were a constant reminder that I was not alone on this journey. Their unwavering support provided me with strength and encouragement, reassuring me that we were in this together, even if physically apart. The virtual calls and messages that we exchanged helped bridge the distance, and I could feel their love reaching me through the screens.

As the days passed, I noticed a transformation within myself. The prolonged isolation provided an opportunity for self-reflection and growth. I learned to appreciate the simple joys and blessings in life, discovering newfound gratitude for health, the support of loved ones, and the beauty of each day.

Their acts of kindness not only lifted my spirits during those challenging days but also left a lasting impact on my heart. I realized the true meaning of family and friends and the depth of their love for me. Their presence in my life became a source of inspiration and gratitude, as their support became a tangible expression of the love that surrounded me, both from my family and friends but most importantly from God.

As I eventually recovered and returned to work, I carried with me the lessons learned during those challenging fifty-seven days. I was grateful that my bills continued to be paid with the money from Kenny's work equipment that had been sold. My faith had been strengthened, my perspective shifted, and my heart opened to the beauty of life's intricacies. The profound experiences of encountering God's love and the unwavering support of my family during my COVID journey left an indelible mark on my soul. It was a time of physical and emotional struggles, where my faith was put to the test. Yet, I emerged from the ordeal with a deeper understanding of the presence of God in my life and the profound impact of human connection.

While the pandemic brought immense suffering and loss to many, it also highlighted our collective resilience and the importance of unity in facing such challenges. It spurred innovation in remote work, telemedicine, and virtual communication, accelerating technological advancements. Additionally, it encouraged a reevaluation of our priorities and a deeper appreciation for essential workers who kept society functioning.

Throughout the pandemic, I witnessed countless acts of kindness and selflessness, which reaffirmed my belief in the goodness of humanity. The collective response to the crisis, the tireless efforts of healthcare workers, and the sacrifices made by many to protect others filled me with gratitude and admiration.

As I expressed my thanks to God, I also recognized the importance of cherishing the small joys that brightened each day. The warmth of a smile behind a mask, waving at someone through a glass door, the laughter during virtual gatherings, and the beauty of nature that provided solace during lockdowns became treasures to be thankful for.

The pandemic reminded me that life is precious and unpredictable, urging me to embrace each moment fully. It taught me to value the presence of loved ones, appreciate the support of friends, and find strength in unity, even when physically apart.

As we slowly emerged from the pandemic's grip, I vowed to carry the spirit of gratitude with me into the future. In both moments of ease and prosperity, as well as during times of difficulty and uncertainty like the COVID pandemic, I find solace in embracing the power of gratitude. This simple yet profound practice resonates with the words of Psalm 107:1, "Give thanks to the Lord, for he is good; his love endures forever." This scripture reminds me that gratitude has the remarkable ability to elevate ordinary moments into extraordinary blessings, showcasing the enduring love and goodness of the Divine.

Amidst the challenges and trials that life presents, gratitude remains a steadfast companion that resonates with the teachings of 1 Thessalonians 5:18, "Give thanks in all circumstances; for this is God's will for you in Christ Jesus." It reminds me of the beauty that surrounds us, even during difficult times, and encourages me to find reasons for thankfulness in the midst of adversity.

With gratitude, I am able to honor the incredible miracle of existence itself, echoing the sentiments of Psalm 139:14, "I praise you because I am fearfully and wonderfully made." It helps me acknowledge the interconnectedness that binds all souls together, as expressed in Colossians 3:14, "And over all these virtues put on love, which binds them all together in perfect unity." This fosters a sense of unity and understanding even in the face of life's challenges.

Each day becomes an opportunity to express thankfulness for the countless gifts, big and small, that grace our lives, echoing the words of James 1:17, "Every good and perfect gift is from above, coming down from the Father of the heavenly lights." Through this lens of thankfulness, even the most mundane experiences become a source of joy and enrichment, aligning with Philippians 4:11-12, "I have learned to be content whatever the circumstances."

During times of uncertainty like the COVID pandemic, gratitude becomes a lifeline that aligns with the teachings of Philippians 4:6-7, "Do not be anxious about anything, but in every situation, by prayer and petition, with thanksgiving, present your requests to God. And the peace of God, which transcends all understanding, will guard your hearts and your minds in Christ Jesus." It reminds me that amidst the chaos, there are still reasons to be thankful: the resilience of healthcare workers, the support of friends and family, and the opportunity for personal growth despite the challenges.

Ultimately, this practice of gratitude is deeply rooted in the acknowledgment of a higher power, often referred to as God's grace. It serves as a reminder that even in the face of hardship, there is a greater purpose guiding our journey, echoing Romans 8:28, "And we know that in all things God works for the good of those who love him, who have been called according to his purpose." With a heart full of thankfulness and a soul inspired by this grace, I embrace each day with renewed hope and a sense of purpose, echoing the sentiment of Psalm 118:24, "This is the day the Lord has made; let us rejoice and be glad in it."

In essence, gratitude is a transformative force that shapes my perspective, allowing me to find beauty and meaning in all circumstances, in accordance with the teachings of Philippians 2:14-15, "Do everything without grumbling or arguing, so that you may become blameless and pure, children of God without fault in a warped and crooked generation." It's a practice that empowers me to see the extraordinary in the ordinary and to navigate life's journey with a sense of awe, humility, and appreciation, echoing the words of Psalm 34:1, "I will extol the Lord at all times; his praise will always be on my lips."

Pandemic

JML23

Forgiveness and the Return to My Call

Romans 11:29

For God's gifts and His call are irrevocable. He never withdraws them when once they are given, and He does not change His mind about those to whom He gives His grace or to whom He sends His call.

After my COVID trial and much prayer Nathaniel, Jenn, Ed, and my family of faith encouraged me often to honor Kenny's memory and carry his love and legacy with ongoing outreach. I had so many mixed feelings about what I should do. One day I hesitantly took some of Kenny's clothing to a facility Kenny and I had spoken at. A young man greeted me at the locked doors, let me in and assisted me with carrying the overstuffed bags. He stopped me in the foyer and asked me how I was handling my loss. Tears leaked down my eyes as I told him it was difficult and that I didn't know if God wanted me to continue with the ministry. He kindly put his hand on my shoulder, and He said, "Jody, let me encourage you. Just because Kenny passed does not mean God revoked your call. He just changed your testimony," and then he recited Romans 11:29: "For God's Gifts and his call are irrevocable." (God wink)

When you are committed to fulfilling God's Purpose, there is a way that it is going to be revealed to you. Most of the time, your purpose is revealed to you through your pain. When you know who you are and whose you are, then there is nothing that happens in your life by accident.

Whether you're going through something big or small, pain is an ever-present constant in your life. But you never have to struggle with finding a purpose behind your pain. Take comfort and solace in the timeless words of James 1:2-4, and discover the purpose behind your pain.

James 1:2-4: "Consider it pure joy, my brothers and sisters, whenever you face trials of many kinds, because you know that the testing of your faith produces perseverance. Let perseverance finish its work so that you may be mature and complete, not lacking anything."

God's will is not that you simply suffer aimlessly, randomly, or mindlessly but that you suffer for the purpose of doing good and, more importantly, that you endure that suffering. God does not orchestrate purposeless suffering in your life but rather, on the contrary, redeems your suffering, giving you the grace to endure it for the purpose of serving as a witness to the power of the gospel. People—our children, our spouse, our friends, our boss, our extended family, even skeptical nonbelievers—will observe the way we handle suffering, and they'll learn from us. When they see us endure the same kind of hurts and hardships they experience while remaining humble, faithful, and prayerful before God, they'll pay close attention, curious about the source of our strength.

Nothing testifies to the deep, authentic reality of God's presence in the life of a believer like watching that believer keep their eyes on Jesus while enduring hell on earth. Observing a Christian cry out to God in confusion, pain, and anger, while maintaining the faith to keep calling, to keep weeping, to keep reaching out in hope and trust, is perhaps the greatest apologetic for the Christian faith the world will ever see. Our suffering has the power to change those who are watching us suffer.

What are you going through today? Are you grieving in hope, suffering in hope, wrestling, and struggling and crying in hope? I want to encourage you, tell the Lord that you trust Him no matter what road He asks you to walk. Then praise Him for a growing faith that is more precious than gold.

So there is always a purpose in our pain, and that ultimately is to give all the glory to God.

Faith is an expectation. Faith enables me to wake up in the morning knowing that, "Surely goodness and mercy will follow me all the days of my life." And since this is one of the days of my life, Goodness and Mercy are my bodyguards. One on my right, and one on my left. You can't see them, they're invisible, but if you look real close, we've got security. Goodness and mercy.

I hold on to that meeting and the assurance that God's love continues to be ever-present. God's love is unwavering and unchanging, His presence is constant, and His plan, though often mysterious, is rooted in His infinite wisdom.

And so yes, I pressed forward, with perseverance.

In the midst of that unimaginable pain, Jesus was there. His presence enveloped me, offering strength amidst the chaos and confusion. His love became the anchor that held me steady amidst the storm, a source of comfort when my world seemed to crumble.

As I walked into the hospital, burdened with grief and a heavy heart, Jesus walked with me every step of the way. He provided the courage to face the heartbreaking reality before me and the wisdom to navigate the difficult decisions that lay ahead.

In that hospital room, surrounded by the beeping machines and the hushed whispers of medical staff, I leaned on Jesus' grace and guidance. I found the strength to make the difficult choices, knowing that His love encompassed both Kenny and me, no matter the outcome.

Through tears and prayers, I surrendered to His will, placing my trust in His divine plan. The road ahead was excruciatingly painful, but I clung to the assurance that Jesus was there, holding me tightly in His embrace.

In the days that followed, as I grappled with grief, Jesus, my family, and my closest friends became my source of encouragement. Their love permeated the darkest corners of my anguish, gently guiding me towards acceptance and granting me the strength to carry on.

Though the pain and loss were immeasurable, I found solace in knowing that Jesus understood the depths of my sorrow. His presence, unwavering and steadfast, provided the support I needed to navigate the tumultuous waves of grief and forge a path towards healing.

In the months and years that followed, I continued to lean on Jesus' love, drawing from His wellspring of grace and finding the courage to rebuild my life. He remained by my side, offering comfort and strength as I sought to piece together the fragments of my shattered heart.

Through the anguish and the tears, Jesus became my constant companion in the journey of healing. His presence transformed my grief into a testament of resilience and a reminder that even in the darkest moments, His light never fades.

As I reflect on that guttural scream and the pain that followed my loss, I am reminded of Jesus' sacrifice. Jesus, the Son of God, who willingly chose to endure immense suffering on the cross to redeem humanity and reconcile them with God.

During his final hours before crucifixion, Jesus experienced deep grief and sorrow. In the Garden of Gethsemane, he prayed fervently, feeling the weight of what was to come. The Gospels mention that he was "greatly distressed and troubled" (Matthew 26:37) and said, "My soul is overwhelmed with sorrow to the point of death" (Matthew 26:38). This moment shows Jesus' human nature, where he grappled with the impending sacrifice and the physical and emotional pain it would entail.

On the cross, Jesus endured unimaginable suffering, bearing the sins of the world. Amidst the agony, he displayed remarkable compassion, asking God to forgive those who crucified him, saying, "Father, forgive them, for they know not what they do" (Luke 23:34). His sacrifice exemplified unparalleled love, demonstrating the extent to which he was willing to go for the sake of humanity's redemption.

The combination of Jesus' sacrifice and his own grief serves as a profound example of selflessness, compassion, and the depth of divine love. It remains a cornerstone of Christian faith, symbolizing hope, forgiveness, and the promise of eternal life.

I cling to our shared mission with renewed determination. I made a solemn vow to carry on Kenny's legacy, to honor his memory by continuing the work we had started together.

Through the depths of my grief, I found strength in the stories of the lives we had touched, the hope we had ignited, in the hundreds of people who attended his calling hours and the transformations we had witnessed in so many lives. I knew that Revolution Ministries had become bigger than the two of us—it had become a lifeline to those yearning for a second chance.

I drew upon the support of our volunteers. My church family rallied behind me and began supporting me in many ways. I had the encouragement of a new spiritual mom, mentor, and friend. Paula. I was blessed with awesome parents, but the Lord has also blessed me with this beautiful woman. She has been a spiritual mother, mentor, and friend.

She had been in my life for many years. She supported Revolution Ministries Akron when it was in the beginning stages. She encouraged me to continue even after the loss of Kenny. She has collected donations for our team, She has sat at my table and helped pack ministry bags, she has prayed with me during some of the hardest times in my life and covers me and so many others with prayer.

Mothers are constantly seeking to encourage growth and development in their children—and children cannot grow and develop without that input. Mothers are constantly affirming their children's attempts to develop new skills. They will push them to do things they can't yet achieve, and be right behind them, ready to catch them when they fall, pick them up, and help them try again. This woman has always projected stability, confidence, and love for me and the body of CHRIST. I know this, I wouldn't know the Lord like I do today if it wasn't for her heart for me.

And the only regret I have is not having her in my life sooner!

Who in your church do people turn to for prayer or a hug when they're hurting? Who do they call at one a.m. the morning? Who in your church is always seeking the best for others, even at her own cost? Who will come running if someone has a need? Who brings the needs of others to your attention? Whose door is always open even to strangers?

This woman does! I also gained five new team members and volunteers. They became an integral part of my strength, reminding me of the importance of our mission and the lives we were impacting.

Together, we recommitted ourselves to making a difference, knowing that Kenny's spirit would guide us every step of the way.

On our first outreach after my husband's death, I felt a mix of emotions as I embarked on this journey alone without my plus one and his protection. The memories of the outreach work we did together flooded my mind, but I knew I had to carry on with our shared mission of reaching out to those in need.

During the outreach, we came across a man whom we had ministered to for over five years. He struggled with addiction that had led him down a tumultuous path, repeatedly finding himself trapped in the cycle of substance abuse, alcoholism, and spending time behind bars. Previously, we were able to provide him with some guidance and support, but unfortunately, the grips of addiction proved to be too strong.

As fate would have it, we encountered him again and when he asked where the big man was, "Kenny," I vividly remember my response. I was prepared for questions about my husband, but never imagined having to explain his death and its cause the very first time we resumed our efforts. It was a heart-wrenching moment, and I questioned why God would allow this to happen.

Yet, with all the pain, I found strength in sharing his story. I trusted that God's plan would encompass both joy and sorrow, and through our outreach, I had to find the strength to explain that Kenny had relapsed and tragically passed away due to an overdose.

Witnessing the anguish on the man's face, it was a stark reminder of the devastating consequences of addiction and how it can affect not just the individual but also those around them, including those he tried to help.

From that moment onward, I knew my new testimony would be centered around the importance of understanding the gravity of addiction and its potential to claim lives. I wanted to share my story, be vigilant and empathetic toward those struggling with addiction, to offer a helping hand instead of judgment. Allowing them to know although Kenny looked strong One more time of using drugs could cost someone their life, and it reminds me it is crucial to intervene, offer support, and advocate for rehabilitation.

Though my heart weighed heavy with grief, I found solace in the moments when my feet hit the ground during the outreach. Boots on the ground if you will. An overwhelming sense of peace washed over me, as if my late husband's spirit was guiding and supporting me in this mission. It had been years since we had seen someone accept Christ during our outreach work, but on that fateful day, God honored me with the incredible privilege of witnessing a life-changing salvation.

This encounter reaffirmed my belief in the power of hope and redemption. Despite the pain and challenges faced, the potential for transformation and renewal lies within us all. It was a reminder that our work in reaching out to others, extending love, compassion, and understanding, can have a profound impact on someone's life.

As I continue to carry on our outreach work, I do so with a renewed sense of purpose. My experience with the man struggling with addiction serves as a driving force and I still hold on to the belief that through God's grace and love, there is always hope for healing and new beginnings, no matter how dire the circumstances may seem.

I poured my heart and soul into expanding the reach of the Revolution Ministries as we opened our hearts to God's guidance and remained obedient to His call. He graciously gifts us with words of knowledge and orchestrates chance meetings. Through His Holy Spirit, He imparts wisdom, understanding, and discernment to us, enabling us to speak words of encouragement, hope, and healing to those in need.

These divine encounters may seem coincidental or random, but they are evidence of God's hand at work. He brings people across our paths for specific reasons, allowing us to be vessels of His love and compassion in their lives.

In these moments, we may find ourselves speaking words we didn't even know we possessed, providing comfort to someone struggling with their faith, or offering guidance to a person facing challenges. God's wisdom flows through us when we humbly submit ourselves to His leading.

Being attuned to God's voice through prayer and seeking His presence in our daily lives helps us recognize the opportunities He presents. It's a beautiful partnership, where we willingly yield to His guidance, and He empowers us to impact others in profound ways.

Through these divine appointments, we witness God's incredible ability to work through ordinary people like us, transforming lives and spreading His light throughout the world. It's a testament to His boundless grace and the significance He places on using each of us to fulfill His divine purposes.

Drawing upon Kenny's experience and the lessons he had taught me, I dedicated resources to continuing our mission and empowering those we encountered to reclaim their lives and fulfill their potential.

A year had passed since Kenny's passing. I had started attending a new church when he had relapsed to allow him to attend church with his family.

My choice to leave during his struggles had caused others to place blame on me for his death, which resulted in the alienation of my then church community, and some of his grieving family which at one time rallied behind Kenny, Nathaniel, and me.

In the depths of my heart, I found myself repeatedly searching, questioning if I inadvertently hurt or offended someone while grappling with my own grief. The burden of uncertainty weighed heavily, and I yearned for reassurance that my actions were never misguided during such a vulnerable time. The need to seek forgiveness and understanding became a constant companion on this journey of self-reflection and healing.

This began to cause immense heartache and bitterness, leaving me grappling with the loss of not just my husband but also vital connections that once brought us together. I hoped that time and understanding would eventually pave the way for healing and reconciliation. The Lord spoke to me after his death about delivering gifts to His mother and stepfather for every holiday following His passing, I faithfully followed The Lord's guidance.

Despite my efforts, they chose not to reconcile the broken relationship. I trust that I fulfilled the Lord's wishes and hope that healing and understanding may come in the future. But after many failed attempts I had to resort to leaving it all in the Lord's hands.

Unforgiveness, bitterness, and resentment act as formidable jailers, keeping us imprisoned within our own pain and suffering. These negative emotions become shackles that restrain us from moving forward and experiencing true emotional freedom. As we cling to grudges and refuse to forgive, we become trapped in a cycle of hurt and negativity, isolating ourselves from the possibility of healing and growth.

In contrast, forgiveness and gratitude are the keys that unlock those heavy shackles, releasing us from the confines of our own emotional prison. When we choose to forgive, we set ourselves free from the burden of carrying past grievances. It is not a sign of weakness but a courageous act that empowers us to let go of the pain and embrace a brighter future.

Practicing gratitude further amplifies the liberating effect of forgiveness.

Gratitude shifts our focus from dwelling on what we lack or what has hurt us to acknowledging the abundance of goodness and blessings in our lives. It helps us see the silver linings even in challenging circumstances, allowing us to find strength and hope amidst difficulties.

As we release the grip of unforgiveness and cultivate gratitude, the healing process begins. Forgiveness offers a path to inner peace and emotional well-being. It restores harmony within us and allows us to rebuild damaged relationships with others. This newfound sense of peace attracts positive energy and blessings, creating a ripple effect that enhances our overall well-being.

Through forgiveness and gratitude, we embark on a journey of transformation. We learn valuable lessons from our past experiences, which become steppingstones for personal growth and resilience. Instead of being confined by our pain, we become liberated by the power of forgiveness, paving the way for a life filled with blessings, joy, and authentic connections with others.

In conclusion, unforgiveness, bitterness, and resentment hold us captive in our own pain, but forgiveness and gratitude provide the keys to unlock the shackles. By embracing forgiveness and cultivating gratitude, we free ourselves from the confines of negativity, allowing healing and blessings to follow in abundance. It is a transformative journey that empowers us to reclaim our lives and find the path to a more fulfilling and joyful existence.

The weight of his loss lingered heavily in my heart, and in the depths of my despair, I turned to Jesus once again. With tears streaming down my face, I fervently prayed. I began to thank God for the support system he had now placed in my life. They were such an amazing part of Revolution Ministries. He brought alongside me a powerful team of pastors, intercessors, prophets, and evangelists. I thanked him for the miracles, healing, and salvation we had encountered and witnessed.

During this prayer my heart turned as I prayed that the lord forgive me for the unforgiveness that had taken root in my heart. I prayed for all involved and I even found myself praying for the man who had supplied Kenny with the last drugs that ended his life. That he would be blessed and not carry any burden of shame or guilt but find a path to full recovery.

Little did I know that divine intervention was already at play. Unbeknownst to me, the man had sought help at a treatment center tucked away in my very own backyard. The treatment center I had just emailed about being a referral source when we came in contact with someone who needed recovery help. The universe had aligned our paths, guided by an unseen force.

Then, my phone buzzed with an unexpected message. It was him, the man I had prayed for, reaching out to me. He shared his incredible journey of transformation, revealing that he had relocated to North Dakota and rebuilt his life from the ground up. He spoke of his steady employment and, most importantly, his newfound sobriety, which had endured for two years.

As I read his words, tears welled up once again. (A God wink.) But this time, they were tears of joy and profound gratitude. Kenny's passing had not been in vain. The echoes of his struggle had reached deep into the man's soul, triggering a desire for change, for redemption.

In his message, the man expressed sincere remorse for the role he had played in Kenny's tragedy. With each passing day, this man's testimony continued to prove that the darkness of addiction could be conquered, his story serving as a powerful reminder that even the deepest wounds could heal, and those burdened with guilt could find redemption.

In time, we realized that Kenny's spirit lived on through our collective efforts. His memory became a symbol of strength, reminding us all to cherish life's precious moments and embrace the opportunity for change.

And so, as the years rolled on, the mission flourished. We touched lives, mended broken spirits, and served people not only physically but spiritually. Kenny's death, though tragic, had become a catalyst for a revolution of hope and healing—a legacy that would forever echo in the hearts of those who knew his story.

My heart was heavy one morning with the weight of losses I had endured. Grief and loss is like a roller coaster. I know it is cliche, but it is the honest truth. Now the enemy had come against my finances, and I yearned for answers and restoration.

As I traveled along a local highway, I found myself in deep contemplation, asking the Lord for guidance and peace. I prayed with all my heart, seeking reassurance that brighter days were coming and that the pain of my losses would be totally healed.

I asked the Lord when He would restore what I had lost and yearned for a sign, a reassurance that He was listening. If I could I would take all of my finances and put them into ministry.

I remember a time that I would travel this route daily, and the enemy many times tried to take me out. He did so by causing three broken windshields, by construction barrels rolling out in front of me, and semi-trucks drifting into my lane.

I thanked the Lord for his protection and realized later that those exact routes took us to a new territory for outreach. Right where the enemy attacked me is the exit we get off of to go minister.

Tears of gratitude welled up in my eyes as I felt a sense of peace and hope washing over me. In that moment, I knew that the Lord had heard my prayers and that, in time, He would indeed restore what I had lost.

Massillon and Canton have become a place of spiritual significance for me, a place where I have found solace, and a place where I felt the divine presence guiding me. What the enemy meant for harm, God turned into good. And the moment my feet hit the ground for outreach I was overcome by the presence of the Holy spirit.

The losses I had endured were all replaced with new opportunities and unexpected blessings. Over the next two years, Revolution Ministries continued to thrive and expand, carrying Kenny's legacy forward. Enlarging our territory and placing us in Canton, one of Ohio's worst cities known for crime. God infused every blessing bag we distributed, every hand we held, and every life we touched and became the driving force behind my unwavering commitment to serving those in need.

Through it all, I know that Kenny's struggle was used for good. His battle with addiction, though tragically cut short, had inspired a movement of compassion, understanding, and hope. I was determined to ensure that his name would forever be associated with love and transformative change.

Forgiveness

Purpose

Matthew 6:33-34

But seek first his kingdom and his righteousness, and all these things will be given to you as well. Therefore do not worry about tomorrow, for tomorrow will worry about itself. Each day has enough trouble of its own.

In this chapter, I'm going to share with you about my vocation and how God put my life in motion over twenty-five years ago when I became a nursing assistant.

I found great understanding when I realized God didn't only want me to become a caregiver and servant but also a confidant to many of the individuals under my care. As I developed deep connections with them, they often felt comfortable enough to share their deepest fears, regrets, and cherished memories with me.

Being entrusted with their innermost thoughts and feelings was both humbling and heartwarming. I became a receptacle for their life stories, struggles, and triumphs. For some, after hours of care, I was the only person they felt they could confide in, as they grappled with the challenges of aging and the complexities of life.

The weight of the stories shared by those who lived through world wars was even more profound. The context of war added an extra layer of gravity to their experiences, as they navigated through the uncertainties and hardships of conflict.

The accounts of some of the veterans I cared about were horrendous. Being held captive prisoners reflected the harsh realities faced by many individuals caught in the midst of armed conflicts. These stories highlighted the immense challenges of captivity, the resilience required to survive, and the emotional toll it took on those involved. Such narratives served as reminders of the importance of peace and diplomacy in preventing such tragic circumstances.

This reminded me of one notable war from biblical times where people overcame incredible odds is the Battle of Jericho, during the conquest of Canaan by the Israelites led by Joshua.

Jericho was a heavily fortified city with impenetrable walls, making it a formidable opponent. However, the Israelites followed divine instructions: they marched around the city walls for six days, and on the seventh day, they marched around it seven times. When they blew their trumpets, the walls miraculously collapsed, allowing the Israelites to overcome the city and claim victory.

The Battle of Jericho is often cited as a powerful example of faith, perseverance, and the belief in divine intervention during biblical times.

My clients shared the struggles of pregnant women with no protectors at home during wartime shedding light on the sacrifices made on the home front. These women displayed incredible strength as they faced the anxieties of war while nurturing new life within them. Their stories spoke to the resilience and adaptability of mothers and families during tumultuous times.

The iconic imagery of Rosie the Riveter working in the aircraft industry symbolized the transformation of societal roles during war. Women stepped up to fill vital roles in the workforce, contributing significantly to the war effort. Their dedication and hard work played a crucial role in supporting the troops overseas and ensuring the continuity of vital industries.

Amidst the chaos of war, the stories of those working on farms from dusk to dawn offered glimpses of stability and determination. Farmers became the backbone of food production, ensuring that the nation's sustenance remained intact during difficult times. Their tireless efforts showcased the resilience and selflessness of those on the home front.

Listening to these stories about war times served as a stark reminder of the human cost of conflict. It underscored the importance of understanding the consequences of war on individuals, families, and communities. These narratives also emphasized the significance of unity and support during challenging periods, fostering a sense of unity and togetherness.

As a young woman hearing these stories, I felt a deep sense of gratitude for the sacrifices made by previous generations. These accounts ignited a desire in me to carry forward the lessons learned, working towards a future where understanding and compassion prevail over conflict.

Their openness demonstrated the level of trust they had in me, and I treated their revelations with utmost respect and confidentiality. I listened with empathy and without judgment, providing a safe space for them to express their emotions.

These intimate moments allowed me to understand their unique perspectives, which in turn helped me tailor their care to their individual needs. By knowing their personal histories, I could approach their medical and emotional care more holistically, fostering a deeper sense of connection and understanding.

Becoming a mentor to many was not a role I had initially anticipated, but it became an integral part of the caregiving process. It taught me the value of active listening and the impact of human connection in the healing process. Through their stories, I learned valuable life lessons and gained a profound appreciation for the resilience of the human spirit.

In those moments of vulnerability, I realized the significance of my presence in their lives, beyond the tasks of daily care. I was not just a caregiver, but also a source of companionship and emotional support during their journey through aging.

Reflecting on these experiences, I can say that being a nursing assistant has enriched my own life. Their stories and trust have left an indelible mark on my heart. It is a constant reminder to me of the privilege and responsibility it takes to be a compassionate caregiver and that the world should continue to honor and respect the elderly.

One of the very first things you are taught in your nursing studies is to not engage in personal discussions about your own life. However, over time, strong bonds may develop between the caregiver and the individual receiving care. This bond can be so profound that they often begin to feel like family. Being seen as family can be a positive aspect of caregiving, as it can create a sense of comfort and trust for the individual receiving care.

Which brings me to Delores. She was a remarkable woman I had the privilege of caring for at a rehabilitation center. At times, she would feel incredibly lonely and would press her call light multiple times seeking companionship. I always made sure to respond promptly and engage her with genuine care and compassion, especially during the quiet nights when loneliness seemed to hit her the hardest.

As we spent time together, I discovered a beautiful connection between us. She shared her life with me. She shared nursing stories. She shared her heartaches. After her rehabilitation, we stayed in touch. Years later her family reached out to me when Delores made the decision to choose hospice care due to a terminal illness. It was an honor to become her companion during this challenging time.

During our time together, Delores became not just a patient but also a dear friend, a Bible study partner, and a spiritual mother figure to me. Her wisdom, faith, and kindness enriched my life profoundly. This experience had a lasting impact on me, sparking a deep interest in hospice care and the significance of providing emotional support and companionship to those facing the end of life.

Delores had a heart full of love and admiration for not just me but also my husband Kenny and Nathaniel. She cherished our relationship and always supported our journey in ministry. Her encouragement and unwavering faith in us were a source of strength, especially during challenging times.

When we embarked on our first missions, Delores's family was the first to extend their support, showing their generosity through donations of socks for those we sought to help. Their kind gesture touched our hearts deeply and reminded us of the power of compassion and community.

Delores's influence on our lives extended far beyond her time in hospice care. She had a profound impact on my spiritual growth and the way we approached our ministry work. She would at times be vulnerable about the process of dying. She would ask questions like, "Will I remember my family?" Which would have me digging into the scripture to find answers for her. I am forever grateful for the privilege of knowing her and for the lessons she taught me about the true meaning of care, connection, and the importance of giving back. Her daughters still reach out to me to this day, and we share in her memories.

Another client who had a vast impact on my life was a sweet little man. The experiences he shared with me as a POW was a deeply profound and personal story. I was enamored that he entrusted me with such pain. He revealed a side of his life that he had never shared with anyone else before.

During our conversations, he affectionately called me his "blue-eyed girl." His granddaughter, Anna, often mentioned how he had waited for me on the day he passed into glory. I felt a connection with her during our time together at her grandfather's bedside. It was a cherished bond that touched both our lives in a meaningful way.

Over a year after his passing Anna reached out to me. She was now the branch manager of the hospice company. She was deeply moved by the compassionate care I provided for her sweet grandfather during his final days. She always complimented my dedication and kindness during the process of his passing. Maybe I had left a lasting impression on her and her family as she extended a job opportunity as a hospice aide. I was not looking for a job. But she believed I would be an invaluable addition to the team, providing the same level of care to other patients in need.

You never know who is watching you.

She noticed over the years the depth of my empathy and the power of my faith, and she saw in me the potential to provide spiritual support and comfort to those nearing the end of life's journey.

After dedicating twenty-five years of hard work as a nursing assistant, the toll on my body became evident. Two years into this position the physically demanding nature of the job took its toll, and unfortunately, I suffered a back injury. The years of lifting and assisting patients had caught up with me, leaving me facing the challenge of managing the pain and seeking medical help. Despite the injury, I cherish the meaningful connections I made with patients and the satisfaction of knowing I made a difference in their lives. Now I had to begin focusing on my recovery and exploring new paths to continue contributing to the healthcare field in a less physically taxing capacity.

Anna offered me a position in the office to accommodate my medical condition until I could be medically cleared for regular duties. During this process we were also going through an acquisition, and our company was bought out. Her understanding and willingness to support me during this challenging time were greatly appreciated, and I am grateful for the opportunity she provided me to continue contributing to the team in a safe and manageable manner. Her kindness and empathy made a significant difference in my work experience during that period.

In the midst of my own healing journey and the ministry's outreach, she then offered me the opportunity to serve as a chaplain in the context of hospice care—a calling that resonated deeply within me for years. It was a chance to accompany individuals and their families through their most vulnerable moments, offering spiritual guidance, a listening presence, and prayers of peace.

God was in the habit of doing things suddenly in my life. With a heart full of gratitude and a renewed sense of purpose, I embraced the role, knowing that it was a divine appointment.

As a chaplain in hospice, I entered homes and care facilities, walking alongside patients and their families during this sacred transition. As you know I myself had lived through similar experiences. I hoped to be a comforting presence, a compassionate ear, and a space for reflection, prayer, and spiritual connection.

Being a hospice chaplain has been a truly eye-opening experience for me. I believe the loss of my husband, grandmother, and many others in the past had given me a unique perspective that allowed me to deeply sympathize with our clients and their families.

You see, going through personal loss has made me realize the complexities of grief and the array of emotions that come with it. This understanding enables me to connect with our clients on a much deeper level and create a safe space where they can freely express their feelings and fears during their loved ones' end-of-life journey.

I've learned that everyone copes with death differently, and that's why I approach each person with utmost sensitivity, always respecting their individual beliefs, cultural backgrounds, and spiritual outlooks.

Experiencing loss has also shown me how crucial companionship and spiritual support are during tough times. Through my own journey of healing, I've discovered the power of active listening and the importance of being fully present with others.

Although very difficult, my own personal experiences have equipped me with valuable coping strategies and insights, which I share with those who are going through similar situations. I find that being able to understand the complexities of grief has made me a source of inspiration and hope for those who may be struggling to find meaning and purpose amidst their pain.

He doesn't call the qualified; he qualifies the called.

I have witnessed many profound moments, the transformative power of faith, the importance of addressing spiritual and emotional needs at the end of life, restoration and reconciliation and that God's love and peace were and are ever-present, even in the face of death.

Through my work as a chaplain, I found a beautiful intersection between my personal journey of healing, the mission of Revolution Ministries, and the calling to provide spiritual care to those in the midst of their own losses.

In the quiet moments at the bedside, I also witnessed the courage, grace, and resilience that often arise during this profound time. Through the intertwining threads of grief, faith, and hope, the ministry and my role as a hospice chaplain only amplified the impact of Jesus on my life.

In my role as a chaplain, I have come to realize that one of the most significant challenges people face on their sickbed is unforgiveness. Over the course of my twenty-five years as a nursing assistant, I have encountered numerous stories where patients grapple with the burden of holding onto grudges and unresolved conflicts. These emotions can weigh heavily on their hearts, hindering their ability to find peace and healing, not only of emotions and spirit but also of our physical bodies.

I've observed that many individuals also fear that they may have neglected to repent for things unknown, carrying a sense of guilt or regret. In such vulnerable moments, they yearn for spiritual solace and the opportunity to seek forgiveness, both from others and themselves.

Sharing a simple prayer with my clients, where I have them repeat with me stating, "Lord, forgive me of any known or unknown sins," seems to have a profound impact on their transition from this life to the next. It appears that this act of acknowledging and seeking forgiveness creates a sense of peace and closure for my clients. By embracing vulnerability and humbly seeking forgiveness, coupled with the power of prayer can be deeply healing and transformative, making the transition process a more serene and spiritually uplifting experience for all who are involved. I have witnessed the transformative power of forgiveness, helping patients find closure, release their burdens, and embrace a sense of spiritual healing.

Throughout my journey, I have learned that acknowledging the significance of forgiveness and repentance can greatly impact a patient's overall well-being during their time of illness. Each story I've encountered has reinforced the importance of empathy, love, and forgiveness in the healing process, both for patients and their families. As I continue my work, I remain committed to fostering an environment of compassion and understanding.

Jesus became the guiding light of my visions in my vocation. His example of reaching out to the marginalized, offering healing to the broken, and embracing the outcasts resonated deeply within my heart.

I sought to emulate Jesus' empathy and understanding, treating each person I encountered with dignity and respect. I began to listen, not just with my ears but with my heart, as I walked alongside those transitioning to be with

Jesus, trapped in poverty, homeless, or trapped in addiction. I strived to be His hands and feet, extending compassion, and offering a glimmer of hope in their darkest life events and realized sometimes this is just being the ministry of presence in someone's struggles.

I recognized that true transformation lay not only in providing physical care but in fostering spiritual growth and healing. I learned to offer prayer in the moment, I shared testimonies of hope, and pointed individuals toward Jesus. The only healer, the only comforter, the only deliverer, the only one that could possibly bring peace in the midst of any trial.

Jesus should serve as our moral compass. His teachings reminded me to challenge systemic injustices, to speak out against stigmatization, and to fight for access to resources and opportunities. I will always want to create a society where the principles of love and compassion guide decisions, just as they did in Jesus' ministry.

Hospice care is indeed a vital service that provides comfort, support, and dignity to individuals with terminal illnesses. However, despite its noble purpose, there are still misconceptions and misunderstandings surrounding hospice in society. Some people may wrongly associate hospice with some form of euthanasia, which is entirely inaccurate. In reality, hospice care focuses on enhancing the quality of life for patients who are already in the final stages of their illness, rather than hastening their passing.

These misconceptions can lead to stigmatization and fear, making it challenging for some individuals and families to opt for hospice care when it could greatly benefit their loved ones. Raising awareness and understanding about the true nature of hospice is essential to combatting this stigma and allowing more people to access the compassionate care they deserve during their final days. By shedding light on the comforting and supportive aspects of hospice, I can only hope to see a shift in societal perceptions towards this crucial end-of-life care option.

I discussed one aspect of finding peace during the process of repentance at life's end. Now let me reflect on the importance of seeking forgiveness and making amends.

I will share a story of forgiveness that I often share with those in the last stage of their terminal illness. This story reminds us that forgiveness can be a transformative and healing force, capable of bringing full healing and redemption.

Over the course of a remarkable twenty-five-year career as a nursing assistant and throughout my career, I have found myself constantly drawn to engaging with clients who may have had a disagreeable spirit or demeanor, and it reminds me of the profound teachings of Jesus, who left the ninety-nine to seek out the one. In doing so, I am reminded of the power of compassion and empathy, and the transformative impact it can have on people's lives.

I firmly believe that every individual deserves understanding and support, regardless of their outward demeanor. While it may be more comfortable to interact with agreeable and amiable clients, I feel a strong sense of responsibility to reach out to those who may be difficult or challenging. I see this as an opportunity to demonstrate genuine care and concern.

Behind emotions like anger, bitterness, frustration, and even rage, often lies a concealed layer of deep-seated pain. These intense emotions can act as a protective barrier. Sometimes its manifestation is truly someone just struggling to cope or communicate their true feelings of hurt, sadness, or vulnerability.

By choosing to engage with these clients, I am essentially embracing the concept of leaving the comfort zone to embrace the path less traveled. It can be daunting at times, as it requires patience, resilience, and an open heart, but the rewards are immeasurable. It is a test for me. Trying to win someone over. Don't get me wrong here, Winning them over doesn't mean manipulating or forcing change upon them, but rather, it is about fostering a connection that allows for personal growth and positive transformation.

Throughout my journey, I have witnessed remarkable changes in some of the most resistant and initially challenging clients. By approaching them with empathy and seeking to understand their underlying struggles, we can often uncover the root causes of their behavior. This deeper understanding allows me to tailor my approach and support them more effectively, ultimately leading to a breakthrough in our relationship.

I find comfort in the idea that my efforts mirror the teachings of Jesus, who cared deeply for all of mankind. He never judged anyone based on their external appearances or behavior; instead, he offered unconditional love and acceptance. Similarly, I strive to extend the same level of compassion and care to everyone I encounter, knowing that the most challenging cases often hold the potential for the most significant impact and later testimony.

It is a journey of empathy, understanding, and patience that leads to transformative growth for both the client and myself. It is a path I choose with purpose and passion, and I wholeheartedly believe in the power of compassion to heal and uplift those who need it the most.

There was a woman whom I cared for deeply. Despite her occasional unpleasant demeanor, I never wavered in my commitment to providing her with the best care possible.

Day after day, I dedicated myself to assisting this woman with her daily needs. I would spend extra time with her, ensuring that her hair was well-tended, and her nails were neatly painted. Through these small acts of kindness, I hoped to bring a touch of joy and comfort to her life, even amidst her moments of bitterness.

Though she wasn't always nice, I understood that everyone's journey is unique, and sometimes, the pain of life's challenges can manifest in unkind behavior. I refused to let her actions deter me from my mission of providing compassionate care.

In my heart, I knew that my role as a nursing assistant extended beyond merely attending to her physical needs. It was about being a steady presence, a source of comfort, and a compassionate listener.

I noticed a change in the woman I deeply cared for. Her demeanor was now clouded with anger, and she lashed out, calling me hurtful names. Surprised and concerned, this constant belittling brought me to tears and I couldn't help but ask her why she was behaving this way. I soon asked her who had hurt her that she would treat me this way.

With a mixture of frustration and vulnerability in her eyes, she finally opened up and shared the root of her pain. Her mother had passed when she was very young. She confided in me that her father had been the one who had been mean to her. That he had been physically and sexually abusive to her until she was eighteen, when she left and never returned or spoke to him again.

Memories of hurtful interactions, neglect, and even abuse seemed to resurface, affecting her emotions in the present moment. As she revealed her past struggles, my heart went out to her. I realized that her outburst wasn't directed at me, but rather a reflection of the unresolved wounds she carried from her past. In that moment, I chose to be a compassionate presence, providing a listening ear and a supportive shoulder.

Despite not yet fully walking in Christ, I felt a deep connection to my faith as a believer. My desire to comfort and help others through prayer was genuine, even if I wasn't entirely sure how to go about it.

When I asked her about her father, I opened a door to a lifetime of pain and unresolved emotions. Her response, revealing that he had been gone for over sixty years, must have weighed heavily on her heart.

Guided by Jesus' teachings of forgiveness and love, I found the courage to speak to her about forgiving her father. She unloaded tears and emotions she had held onto for many years. I recognized that holding onto resentment was keeping her captive and preventing her from experiencing true emotional freedom.

In that moment of vulnerability and divine guidance, I became an instrument of healing and hope. My words and prayers created a safe space for her to confront her feelings and begin the journey towards forgiveness and inner peace.

This encounter shows the power of faith. Even when I felt unsure or imperfect in my beliefs, my sincere intentions and willingness to reach out to others had made a significant difference. It's a reminder that faith is a journey, and my steps towards understanding and walking in Christ's teachings can have a profound impact on those around me.

Understanding that healing from past traumas takes time and patience, I vowed to stand by her side throughout this journey. Together, we began the process of addressing her feelings, helping her find healthier ways to cope with her emotions, and working towards forgiving her father for the pain he had caused.

The next day, as I headed to work and strolled down the corridor to her room, my excitement grew to see her. As I opened her door, my heart sank as I discovered an empty bed. Confused and concerned, I approached the nurses to inquire about what had happened to her.

I had many questions. Had someone gotten her up early? Had she gone to the hospital? Had they changed her room?

With compassion in their eyes, the nurses explained that after I had left the previous day, something remarkable had occurred. She seemed to have experienced a moment of profound happiness, unlike any they had witnessed before. She was speaking with a newfound sense of joy, engaging with other residents and nurses, humming songs in a way that touched their hearts.

The atmosphere around her changed. Little did we know that it was her way of bidding farewell to her beloved companions and caretakers.

Later that night, she quietly slipped away in her sleep, peacefully departing from this world. It was as if she had found contentment and closure, leaving behind her horrific memories. She had finally found peace.

Though I felt a profound sense of loss, I also took solace in knowing that her final moments were filled with joy and that she had touched the lives of those around her in such a beautiful way.

Forgiving those who hurt us allows us to experience a profound sense of healing peace. Through this encounter I learned that we can free ourselves from the burden of hate, resentment, and bitterness, and from the self-inflicted prison we put ourselves in. The act of forgiveness brings undeniable healing to our hearts, enabling us to move forward with greater understanding and empathy. It aligns us with the teachings of Jesus and fosters a deeper connection to the essence of his message—to love one another and let go of the shackles of hatred. Through forgiveness, we open ourselves to the transformative power of grace, experiencing a renewed sense of freedom and inner harmony.

I believe with my act of obedience and the grace of Jesus, this woman delved into the root of her pain. As she confronted her past and found solace in facing her pain, she gradually discovered a sense of peace within herself.

Eventually, she peacefully transitioned to the afterlife, her soul bound for heaven, where she joined Jesus, whom she had grown closer to through her trials and her journey.

Sharing this story with others has had a profound impact, inspiring some to find strength in their own acts of self-forgiveness and healing. And indeed, some have shared that they, too, found peace in their hearts and they shortly transitioned to be with Jesus after carrying huge burdens that kept them bound.

I pray that this story continues to inspire others to embrace their pain, find healing, and grow in faith, knowing that peace and heaven-bound journeys await those who seek Jesus with a sincere heart and forgiveness

Looking back on my journey, I realized that providing care isn't always about receiving kindness in return; it's about recognizing the depth of another person's struggles and being a beacon of support in their darkest hours. While it wasn't always easy, my dedication to my clients' well-being will always be unwavering.

Ultimately, my twenty-five years as a nursing assistant taught me the true essence of companionship and the profound impact it can have on someone's life. My experiences reminded me that even amidst the most challenging circumstances, love, patience, and understanding can create transformative healing and bridge the gap between bitterness and acceptance. It was and is an honor. Her journey along with many others will forever hold a special place in my heart as a testament to the power of healing through Jesus Christ.

Purpose

Healing

Psalm 147:3

He heals the brokenhearted and binds up their wounds.

Two years into my grief, I realized healing, much like a Band-Aid, can be an imperfect process. Sometimes, wounds may initially be covered and protected, but they can still fester beneath the surface. Similarly, emotional and physical healing may take time, and there might be setbacks or moments when it seems like progress is slow.

Even when wounds do heal, they can leave scars as a reminder of the past. Healing from emotional pain or traumatic experiences may not erase the memories completely. Instead, scars, whether physical or emotional, become a part of your story, a testament to the strength and resilience that helped you navigate through difficult times.

Just as a scar might not feel the same as the original wound, it doesn't mean that healing is complete. It involves adapting, growing, and finding a new sense of normalcy. Like a scar, the healing process can bring about changes in your perspective, priorities, and ways of approaching life.

Healing isn't always a linear journey, but it's a testament to your human capacity to mend and transform. Acknowledging that healing takes time, and scars may remain, should foster self-compassion and acceptance. The journey may be challenging, but it can also lead to newfound strength and wisdom, shaping who you are and how you interact with the world around you.

Mourning and having the spirit of grief are related concepts, but they have distinct differences. Mourning is a specific process of expressing sorrow and grief, often in response to the loss of a loved one or something deeply meaningful. It involves outward displays of grief, working through your sadness and finding peace.

On the other hand, having the spirit of grief goes beyond outward expressions and refers to a deeper, emotional state of being. It's a more profound sense of sorrow or sadness that may persist beyond the mourning period and can be experienced in various situations, not just related to death. This emotional state can be caused by various life events, personal struggles, or empathizing with the suffering of others.

Two years had passed since my husband's passing, and as the anniversary approached, the weight of grief still burdened me. The pain was as raw as it was in the beginning, and I found myself asking questions about life's unpredictability and the reasons behind such loss. There were moments when I couldn't hold back the tears, feeling overwhelmed by the emptiness his absence left behind.

During this time, I continued to seek counsel and support from my pastors and mentors, turning to their wisdom and prayers. Their comforting words and guidance offered a glimmer of hope in the darkness.

Despite their support, the journey of healing was ongoing, and I tried to be patient with myself as I navigated through the waves of grief. Each day was a step forward, and then oftentimes many steps back.

In the midst of the grief and approaching anniversary, I decided to plan a vacation hoping to find some joy in life once again. It felt like the right time to take a step back from the heaviness of sorrow.

I eagerly looked forward to being surrounded by my family, my best friend, and my son during this trip. Their presence could possibly help me find a sense of comfort and understanding that I needed. I hoped that being together with them would create new cherished moments and help me find moments of laughter and happiness amidst the pain I was still trying to overcome, honoring the past while also embracing the present and the future.

As I embarked on this journey, I carried the memory of my husband in my heart. I believe vacations heal by offering a break from routine, new experiences, and time for self-reflection, reducing stress and bringing a sense of renewal and energy.

On the second anniversary of Kenny's passing, I made the poignant decision to embark on a journey to a family reunion in the beautiful state of Kentucky, followed by visiting a chapel on a cliff in the Smoky Mountains, a place Kenny and I had always wanted to visit. It had been a staggering seventeen years since I last saw some of my family members.

As I packed my bags, a mix of emotions swirled within me—sadness for the loss of Kenny, but also excitement to reconnect with relatives and revive the bonds that time had momentarily dulled. The reunion brought back cherished memories from my childhood and deep-rooted connections.

The journey felt like a pilgrimage of sorts, as I carried Kenny's spirit in my heart, knowing he would have encouraged me to embrace family ties and find solace in their warmth. As I navigated the winding roads with my best friend, my son, and my nephew, I found comfort in the shared stories, laughter, and love that enveloped the reunion, reminding me that even amidst loss, life's intricate tapestry continued to weave moments of joy and togetherness.

Embarking on a nine-hour drive was an exciting prospect, but it also left me feeling a bit nervous. The thought of an extended road trip filled with new experiences and sights brought a sense of adventure and anticipation. However, the sheer duration of the journey and the responsibility of driving for such a long time triggered butterflies in my stomach.

Excitement bubbled within me, imagining the scenic routes, landscapes, and potential spontaneous stops along the way. The thrill of exploring new places and creating cherished memories with loved ones fueled my enthusiasm.

Yet, the nervousness crept in as I realized the challenges of a prolonged drive. I worried about fatigue, staying alert, flat tires, other drivers, and maintaining focus on the road. Questions about unpredictable weather, road conditions, and potential delays played on my mind, adding to the apprehension.

Despite my nervousness, I reminded myself that the experience would be worth it. As I set off, a mix of excitement and anxiety coexisted within me, propelling me forward on this adventure that promised to be both challenging and rewarding.

In the past, my husband had always taken the wheel on the majority of our vacations, so I knew this was just another step forward in the things I had to overcome.

As I embarked on the nine-hour drive to South Carolina, very spontaneously the heavens opened up, releasing a torrential downpour that seemed relentless. The raindrops danced rhythmically on the windshield, creating a mesmerizing symphony as they splattered against the glass. The once sunny skies were now obscured by dark clouds and wind and it cast an aura of mystery and awe.

The journey took us through the majestic mountains of West Virginia, where the rain's intensity seemed to amplify. At one point, the rain was so heavy that I couldn't even see the road ahead, and it felt like an overwhelming challenge to continue. However, just when it seemed the situation might become insurmountable, an awe-inspiring moment unfolded.

Through the thick curtain of rain, a sight emerged that felt nothing short of miraculous—a semi-truck appeared in front of me, its flashers beaming like guiding lights through the gloom. It felt as though Gods divine hand had intervened, providing some light and direction in the midst of the storm.

With unwavering trust, I followed the semi-truck, guided by its steady presence. The synchronicity of that moment filled me with gratitude and faith, knowing that I was not alone on this challenging journey. As we navigated through the treacherous mountain paths together, the intensity of the rain began to subside, and the clouds above gradually lightened. It was as though the semi-truck had ushered in a sense of calmness and reassurance.

The persistent rain throughout the drive symbolized not only a cleansing but also a refreshing and renewal of the world around me. The raindrops tapping on the car's roof and windows provided a soothing rhythm, almost like a gentle lullaby, lulling me into a contemplative state.

In many spiritual traditions, water is considered a symbol of cleansing and renewal, and that's exactly how the rain felt to me. Just as water cleanses the earth, it is believed to cleanse the soul, washing away impurities and allowing for a fresh start. The rain on that journey seemed to affirm this symbolism, acting as a reminder of the potential for growth and transformation through divine intervention.

It was as if the rain served as God's gentle touch, purifying not only the world around me but also the depths of my own being. The journey through the mountains of West Virginia, guided by the semi-truck's flashers, felt like a metaphorical experience, with the rain acting as a divine blessing, clearing the path for a new beginning.

In the aftermath of the rain, as the sun peeked through the clouds, casting a warm glow over the refreshed landscape, there was an undeniable sense of hope and renewal. The road ahead seemed brighter, and I felt a profound gratitude for the rain's role in the journey.

The experience left me with a lasting impression, a reminder of the interconnectedness of nature and spirituality. It reinforced my belief in a higher power and the profound impact that even the simplest natural occurrences can have on our lives. The rain on that nine-hour drive to South Carolina will forever be a reminder of God's cleansing effect and the potential for spiritual renewal that lies within the most ordinary moments of life.

As that storm raged around me as we traveled, its ferocity and power served as a poignant reminder of how God can be our anchor, providing stability and strength during life's turbulent moments.

Amidst it all, I felt a rekindled peace knowing that just like a lighthouse guides ships through treacherous waters, God's light illuminates our path and helps us navigate through the darkest of times. The storm became a profound symbol of faith, reminding me that with God as our anchor and lighthouse, we can find hope and safety, even in the most challenging circumstances.

Next stop, the picturesque Smoky Mountains of Pretty Place, South Carolina, where we discovered that hidden gem—a charming chapel perched atop a cliff. Its rustic beauty and breathtaking views captivated me instantly. The sight of the chapel seemed to symbolize the intertwining of spirituality and nature, inviting me to contemplate the deeper meaning of our journey.

The healing that unfolded during this initial visit was so profound that I found myself yearning to return. And so we did, not once or twice, but three times during our stay. Each subsequent visit held its own unique magic. As we soaked in the beauty of the mountains, I found solace in the rustling of trees and the chirping of birds.

Though my best friend, son, and nephew occasionally expressed mild boredom, I was grateful for their companionship during these trips. Their presence served as a grounding force, reinforcing the importance of fostering connections and creating memories together.

While my dear companions may not have fully grasped the extent of my emotional journey, the repetitive visits to the Smoky Mountains of Pretty Place. and the chapel atop the cliff became a crossroads of my inner self, where healing and growth converged. The place itself became a living reminder of the significance of returning to our core values and nurturing our souls.

Healing is like revisiting that cross, time and time again, and holds tremendous significance in our lives. Much like the intersection of paths, healing offers us the chance to confront our past wounds, acknowledging their impact, and finding solace in the process. It involves journeying back to moments of pain and vulnerability, unraveling the layers of our emotions, and allowing ourselves to mend and grow stronger.

With each return to that cross, I gained new insights, leading me towards a deeper understanding of myself and my personal growth. Healing becomes a profound and transformative pilgrimage of self-discovery and inner peace, as we embrace the power of transformation at the cross of our being.

Experiencing three days in a row that mirrored the death, burial, and resurrection of Jesus Christ left me in awe and amazement. As I reflected on those moments, I couldn't help but draw parallels to the profound symbolism of renewal and healing that lies within the story of Christ's resurrection. Just as Jesus faced a period of darkness and despair before emerging victorious, I too went through a challenging phase of my own.

During those three days, I felt as though I had encountered my own form of "death"—perhaps symbolizing the struggles and pain that burdened me. It was a time of introspection, where I had to confront my inner demons and face the emotions that had been holding me back. It felt like a spiritual burial, where I had to let go of past hurts and negative influences, allowing myself to be free from their hold.

Yet, within that period of darkness, I found the seeds of transformation taking root within me. Just as Christ's resurrection brought hope and new life, I too experienced a sense of rebirth and rejuvenation. The healing that followed felt like a resurrection of my spirit, a renewal of strength, and a profound sense of peace.

In those three consecutive days, I truly felt the power of renewal and the significance of embracing life after facing adversity. It was a revelation that reminded me of the inherent resilience we possess as human beings. Like Christ's story, my own journey of healing mirrored the cyclical nature of life, where darkness can lead to light, and pain can transform into growth.

This experience left an indelible mark on my soul, and I carry the lessons of those three days with me, cherishing the newfound hope, strength, and gratitude for life's ability to bring about healing and resurrection, just as it did for Jesus Christ.

On the third day of our visit, we were graced by the arrival of my dear friend Jason, who had driven all the way from Alabama to be with us. His presence was incredibly meaningful, as he had been an integral part of both Nathaniel's and my life for over nine years. Since Kenny's funeral, we hadn't had the opportunity to see each other, and his arrival brought a sense of healing and comfort to our hearts.

As we shared stories and memories in the chapel, I couldn't help but feel a profound connection to Jesus' teachings of love, compassion, and forgiveness. It reminded me of the story of the paralyzed man and his friends who lowered him through the roof to be healed by Jesus. Just like the paralyzed man's friends showed incredible faith and determination, Jason and my companions had always been a steadfast support system throughout our journey together.

The memories we created in the Smoky Mountains of Pretty Place remain etched in my mind and heart, and each visit served as a touchstone of healing. As I look back on that trip, I am reminded that life is a continual process of rediscovering ourselves, just like the ever-changing landscape of the mountains.

At the mountaintop chapel, a profound and life-altering experience greeted me. As I entered the sacred space, a sense of tranquility had washed over me, I felt an inexplicable connection to something beyond myself. It was more than just healing; I believe that I encountered a miracle.

The weight of grief that had been resting heavily on my shoulders for what felt like an eternity began to lift. As if touched by divine hands, the spirit of sorrow no longer seemed to hold me captive. It wasn't that the pain vanished entirely, but a newfound sense of peace and hope began to fill the void that grief had left behind.

Much like Jesus at Gethsemane, I found myself in moments of mourning, facing the emotional turmoil that life can bring. However, the encounter at the mountaintop chapel had instilled in me an inner strength, a resilience to endure these trials with a glimmer of faith and a heart open to healing.

In that hallowed space, I sensed the presence of something greater, an overwhelming force of compassion and love that transcended the boundaries of human understanding. It felt as if the universe itself had conspired to lead me to that chapel, where my soul could be touched by grace.

The healing I experienced was not just physical; it was spiritual and emotional, reaching the depths of my being and reshaping my perspective on life. The shackles of grief were loosened, and I found peace in knowing that I was not alone in my struggles.

As days turned into weeks, the transformation within me continued to blossom. The memories of that sacred place sustained me during moments of doubt and despair, serving as a guiding light on my path to recovery.

I still mourn at times, as grief is a natural part of the human experience. But now, I approach those moments with a renewed sense of hope and resilience, much like how Jesus found strength in his moments of anguish at Gethsemane.

In retrospect, I believe that the encounter at the mountaintop chapel was a divine intervention, a miracle that brought healing and light back into my life. It taught me that miracles can happen when we least expect them.

Healing

♥ JML28

The Pardon

Ephesians 1:7

In him we have redemption through his blood, the forgiveness of our offenses, according to the riches of his grace.

Right before my trip, fate intervened. I started chatting with an acquaintance from junior high.

As it turned out, he told me he had been trapped in the religion of the Jehovah Witnesses but recently became a new believer in Christ, experiencing a profound transformation in his beliefs. This newfound faith had led him to explore Christianity more deeply and understand the importance of embracing spirituality. Our conversation shifted from casual chit-chat to heartfelt discussions about our faith, experiences, and the changes we had gone through.

We decided to rekindle our friendship and began to explore our shared spiritual path together, attending church services as a duo. One of the activities that I truly thought strengthened our connection was participating in prayer walks or drives together around the inner cities. We would stop and pray with those we felt the Lord led us to. Our shared faith in Jesus became the driving force behind our activities together, and it felt like our paths had converged for a higher calling.

One night, while we were in church, the Lord blessed me with listening to a powerful testimony and then I received a vision. In this vision, I saw myself holding a bag of mustard seeds. As we embarked on our prayer walks over the inner cities, I felt a divine prompting to sprinkle these mustard seeds along our path. Each tiny seed held a profound meaning, representing our faith and hope in God's transformative grace.

Sprinkling mustard seeds evoked deeper thoughts, those of reaping and sowing, plowing and harvesting. It symbolized the beginning of a cycle of growth and abundance. Just like in life, when we sow seeds of faith, kindness, hard work, and dedication, we can expect to reap the rewards later on. Not for us but for the kingdom of God. It's a reminder that our actions today shape future outcomes, much like the effort put into plowing a field. It will eventually yield a bountiful harvest.

This simple act of sprinkling the seeds served as a powerful metaphor for the interconnectedness of our actions and their consequences. We began praying over bars, strip clubs, adult stores, and I began to feel a deep sense of compassion for the people living in these communities, and a fervent desire for their salvation. The act of sprinkling the mustard seeds symbolized our collective dedication to sowing the seeds of hope and redemption. We believed that every seed scattered would carry the potential to touch someone's heart, leading them closer to the love and salvation of Christ.

During those prayer walks, our unity and shared vision became a powerful force for good. I trusted that God's guiding hand would use these humble actions to bring about positive change, healing, and renewal in the lives of those we prayed for.

In the following days and weeks, we continued to go to church and continued walks and drives, each time with renewed faith and determination, knowing that every mustard seed we scattered represented a soul touched by God's grace. We prayed for the inner cities, believing that our collective efforts, fueled by faith and love, would contribute to bringing forth salvations.

As my trip approached, I felt grateful for the unexpected reunion with my middle school acquaintance and the way our friendship had transformed. We may have started on different paths, but through faith and newfound beliefs, we had come together to share in something truly special. I felt that even with the distance of my upcoming journey, our connection would remain strong, rooted in our shared experiences and mutual understanding of the power of faith.

Throughout my entire vacation, we stayed in contact. Messaging about my healing, the sights we were visiting. I shared my many photos. Meanwhile, my son, after the constant buzzing of message alerts teasingly suggested that we should've just invited him to come along with us on the trip. I couldn't help but chuckle at the thought of it.

What made the situation even more amusing was the irony of it all. This man, who used to mute me on Facebook for the mere mention of Jesus, was now the one initiating conversations about Jesus with me. It was like a complete reversal of roles, and I couldn't help but find it humorous.

Life certainly has a way of surprising us, doesn't it? Who would have thought that someone who once seemed so distant from discussing matters of faith would now be engaging in meaningful conversations and asking many questions about something so important to me? It just goes to show that people can change, and our perspectives can evolve over time.

In the end, I took it all in good stride and appreciated the unexpected turn of events. It served as a reminder that sometimes, the most unexpected connections can lead to the most meaningful exchanges.

After returning from my trip, I reunited with him and we attended a revival together, which was a wonderful experience. During this time, we also started spending more time with my best friend and her husband, which brought us all closer. I noticed that Nathaniel and he began to bond, which was heartwarming to see.

As a group, we began to gather to play cards and engage in Bible studies, fostering a wonderful sense of community and shared experiences. Over time, we affectionately referred to each other as our "tribe," symbolizing the strong bond and connection we all shared.

And "my tribe" humorously coined me "apostle McNugget," injecting laughter and camaraderie into our gatherings.

As time went on, I grew to view him as a close friend, and I was glad to see that he decided to join "Revolution Ministries." It seemed like a great opportunity for spiritual growth and fellowship. We made plans to attend a Christian conference together, and I couldn't resist teasing everyone that maybe I'd meet my future husband there, in a playful and light-hearted manner.

The journey ahead was filled with excitement and anticipation, and I felt blessed to have such wonderful people around me as we embarked on this path together.

The conference was a transformative experience, marked by a powerful outpouring of the Holy Spirit, leaving me feeling spiritually uplifted and invigorated. We were an amazing team. We found ourselves praying with and blessing our waitress' when we ate meals together. It felt like iron sharpening iron.

However, on the second night, amidst the fervent worship and soul-stirring messages, my emotions took an unexpected turn when it came to my friend. Until then, I had never viewed this friendship through a romantic lens; our interactions were always platonic, and we maintained a comfortable distance, even when alone sitting on opposite couches during our discussions.

As the days at the conference passed, I couldn't shake the newfound feelings that were beginning to develop. Conflicted and unsure, I decided to confide in a few close friends and mentors, seeking their guidance and wisdom. They listened attentively and encouraged me to pray about the situation, asking God to reveal His will and provide clarity.

Feeling the weight of uncertainty, I asked my best friend to pray over me during a quiet moment after the conference. I realized just how deep our connection ran and how important he had become in my life. But in the depths of my emotions, I yearned for assurance that the feelings, the butterflies I began feeling when he hugged me, or touched my hand were not merely driven by fleshly desires or fleeting lust, but rather, that they held a deeper significance, a connection to God. Seeking clarity and spiritual understanding, I embarked on a soul-searching journey, hoping to discern the divine essence behind these emotions.

Through our heartfelt conversations over a year, I learned that he had been waiting patiently, praying for reconciliation with a woman with whom he had been in a relationship. I always sensed the sincerity in his voice, and it only deepened my admiration for his faith and resilience.

Intriguingly, as the conference drew to a close, and we returned to our everyday lives, I began having vivid dreams about him. These dreams felt strangely meaningful, almost as if they were trying to convey a message that I couldn't decipher.

Navigating these complex feelings, I continued seeking God's guidance and wisdom, knowing that my friend's heart was tender and had already endured significant pain. While uncertainty still loomed, I held onto the hope that whatever the outcome, God's plan would ultimately prevail and lead us both to where we needed to be.

The conference had left me not only spirit-filled but also heart-stirred, as I grappled with emotions I had not experienced since Kenny's death or expected to encounter within the context of this newfound friendship.

When he made the choice to quit pursuing or rekindling with his ex, it sparked a change within me. I felt a newfound sense of courage and decided to open up my heart to him. I never wanted to interfere with God's Will.

It was a vulnerable decision, but I wanted to share my feelings and the visions and dreams with him, hoping that he would understand the depth of my emotions and the sincerity of my affection.

It was a risk, but I believed that expressing myself honestly was the only way to find out if there was a chance for something more between us. I told him if he didn't feel the same way I would understand.

But after our conversation, he firmly believed that our marriage was destined by God, and he wanted to get married quickly.

After a year of nurturing what I thought was a deep friendship and remarrying, I couldn't ignore the realities that I had disregarded before entering into our covenant. The fact that my partner wasn't employed before our marriage caused me to become the primary breadwinner and it started to weigh heavily on me. Although I initially tried to encourage him to seek a job, it seemed to him like I was nagging, and this created a rift between us.

I longed for him to contribute more to our marriage, not just financially but also in terms of helping with household chores and cooking during his unemployment. While he occasionally found limited work with a friend, it didn't significantly impact our financial situation. It was very seldom, and I felt overwhelmed by the burden of being the sole provider.

The biblical complexities surrounding my understanding of a man as a provider and protector added another layer of confusion and frustration.

I found myself questioning whether I was holding on to outdated beliefs or if there was genuine wisdom in these traditional roles.

Adding to my distress was his continued communication with his ex, which he attempted to keep hidden from me. When I expressed my concerns and tried to talk about it, he accused me of being nosy and crossing boundaries by looking at his phone.

The weight of these challenges began to take a toll on me, and I couldn't help but question the foundation of our marriage. I felt a growing sense of doubt and uncertainty about whether we could overcome these issues and build a fulfilling partnership together.

In this state of turmoil, I knew I needed to reflect on what truly mattered to me in a marriage and whether our values and visions for the future aligned. I sought God in prayer and turned to his holy text for guidance.

Ultimately, I realized that a successful marriage required both partners to be willing to work together, communicate openly, and be respectful of each other's needs and boundaries. It became clear that the current dynamic was not sustainable and that significant changes were necessary for us to move forward.

I mustered the courage to have a candid conversation with my partner about my feelings and concerns. I expressed my need for more support and understanding and addressed the issues of feeling overwhelmed with job responsibilities, communication with his ex, emphasizing the importance of honesty, support, and trust in a marriage.

While the road ahead remained uncertain, there were also the lingering wounds of a thirty-three-year-old childhood trauma that was unexpectedly reopened. A skeleton in my closet and something only my best friend was aware of.

During intimacy It exposed the pain and memories that had long been buried within me. In my marriage to Kenny, my trauma remained unexposed. However, in my new marriage, when this wound surfaced my now husband lacked understanding and empathy, making the healing process challenging and lonely.

Every experience a person has had is stored in the brain, whether it is consciously remembered or not. And the feelings that went along with the experience are also stored in the brain, inseparable from the memory of the experience. Memories replayed like a DVD and continued to affect me in my present situation, often with a negative impact.

It was difficult and painful. Just when I thought I was overcoming, something would trigger a recall. No one likes to open old wounds. We bury them deep; we hide them. Because of this, some people get stuck in survival mode and never get healed.

I realized I could either go through life with a dull, aching pain, or for a brief period go through a crushing pain in order to receive healing.

Self-reliance can be a burden. Hyper vigilance can be a burden. It can make you strive and strain for a mark you'll never hit. Because, guess what? You're not God, and when you are crushed, that is no longer an option. You can't strive because you're too weak. You can't strain for something because you're too broken to do so. And you just have to stop.

When you are in that place of crushing and you have nothing else to give in your own strength, you're left with two choices. You can either depend on God or give up. If you're going to depend on God, your faith is going to get one good workout.

"If dependence upon God is the objective, then weakness is an advantage." How true!

It points us toward God and relieves the pressure of our own performance needing to be enough. It puts the focus where it belongs.

"Jesus."

The rawness of my trauma from the past was casting a shadow over our relationship. The wounds that I thought had healed were brought to the surface, again and again, challenging the foundation of my marriage even more. I began to notice unusual surges of anger rising within me.

During my marriage, there were three instances where I unexpectedly had verbal outbursts and felt the need to defend myself, using harsh words that were even vulgar. On one occasion this was even done in front of a mutual friend. This was very uncharacteristic of me. I started feeling dishonored and disrespected. I felt provoked at times. On one occasion, after an outburst, he decided to leave, returning to stay with the friend he had lived with before moving in with me.

Days went by with not so much as a text message from him. I felt abandoned. I felt misunderstood, undervalued, and unfairly criticized. While it was unlike my usual demeanor, these outbursts were a result of the intense emotions and the desire to protect my self-worth within the relationship.

We have all experienced anger at some point in our lives, and it can be a real problem. Though it starts as a harmless feeling, it can quickly grow into something dangerous that's hard to control.

But with God's help, I assure you we can learn how to deal with our feelings and walk in His peace.

I'll admit, years ago I pretty much did and said anything I felt like. I have a pretty strong personality, so if you said something to upset me, there was a good chance I would let you know about it. But this character had not emerged since I had rededicated my life.

Thank God, that over time God changed me. Through his Word and mentors that helped me, I began to process what I was feeling and began to manage my emotions through the power of His Holy Spirit.

In the midst of hardships I spoke with my spiritual mother, wondering how it was that I couldn't bless my husband when we had an argument—that Jesus had said to bless my enemies, and he wasn't my enemy!

She told me a story about her mother-in-law. She could never please her. She would nag and judge her motives often. And one day the Lord told her to bless her, you know that she likes tea and by the time she would get done boiling water and making the tea, her own anger would be gone. The mother-in-law would then see that she was blessing her, and the nagging would end.

We're all going to be angry at times, but it's not feeling anger that's a problem. The problem comes when we act on those feelings.

At times, I've really wished some of my feelings would go away, but usually they don't. I've learned that God is not necessarily going to change them, but He is going to change me so I can be stronger than they are.

We need to be in touch with our feelings and take responsibility for them, but we can't allow them to control us.

After reflection, I combed through scriptures. One relevant scripture I found about anger was from the book of Ephesians 4:26-27 - "In your anger do not sin: Do not let the sun go down while you are still angry, and do not give the devil a foothold. "

This verse emphasized the importance of handling anger in a righteous manner. While experiencing anger is a natural emotion, it cautions against allowing it to lead to sinful actions. Instead, it encourages resolving conflicts promptly and not letting anger fester, as this could give the devil an opportunity to create division and harm in relationships. Through prayer and introspection, I began to gain clarity and learned to channel my feelings in more constructive ways, even if that meant being silent. I found strength in faith and leaned on patience instead of angry loud outbursts.

Emotions have an uncanny way of rising to the surface, especially anger, which can feel overwhelming and uncontainable. The scars of past experiences lingered, festering beneath the surface, waiting for an opportunity to demand attention.

With a heavy heart and a sincere desire to find healing, I continued to message him and three days later when he answered I asked for forgiveness. However, to my disappointment, when he returned home he still lacked the understanding to truly grasp the turmoil within me.

In moments like these, when vulnerability seeks refuge in compassion, it becomes evident how essential it is to find an anchor amidst the storm.

Yet, this elusive comfort seemed out of reach, as he couldn't comprehend the depth of pain that haunted me. There was a huge void left by his inability to empathize and it became apparent, leaving me feeling even more isolated in my struggle to cope.

Jesus is empathy's perfect example. He didn't come to earth to save us as God, detached and gazing down in sympathy and pity. He came as a man, born into the trenches, to live and suffer as a human. His empathy makes Him the perfect sacrifice. The perfect bridge between God and us.

When we look down into someone else's trench, we shouldn't look down upon them and be critical. We should feel sorrow and sadness; that's sympathy. When we jump into that same trench and get dirty with them that's empathy.

My own situation brought even more clarity. I realized when someone is hurting, we need to allow ourselves to remember the ugliness of our own trenches. What if we, as Christians, were brave enough to open the vault, unlock our own pain, and use it to understand others and follow in Jesus's footsteps?

Empathy doesn't require surviving the exact same situation. Empathy requires a willingness to wear the same emotions. Because no matter what label you slap on your particular trench, it's still a dark and ugly pit. Lonely. Scary. Hopeless. Overwhelming. And a bunch of other destructive adjectives.

If we applied our trench-induced emotions to someone else's trench experience, we could change the church, the world, marriages, and friendships. Empathy is the capacity to feel another person's feelings, thoughts, or attitudes vicariously.

The apostle Peter counseled Christians in 1 Peter 3:8 "to have compassion for one another; love as brothers, be tenderhearted, be courteous." The apostle Paul also encouraged empathy when he exhorted fellow Christians in Romans 12:15 "to rejoice with those who rejoice; mourn with those who mourn."

Within the body of Christ, God doesn't expect us to be everyone's rock. But He draws us to certain people, through life experience and through friendship. I couldn't grasp why he had no understanding or empathy of my turmoil.

I started asking myself, "If you can't do this, but claim to be a Christian, do you truly have the heart of Christ?"

As time went on, I noticed a distressing change in his behavior. He began to say hurtful things. Was it my perception? I often felt provoked when I would say please don't say that or do this because it hurts. I was often left feeling like I was asking for too much.

His words cut deep, chipping away at my self-esteem, and leaving me questioning my own thoughts and emotions. It seemed as though he was dismissive of my feelings and opinions, invalidating everything I expressed. This left me feeling unsure of what was real and what was merely a product of my perceptions. It was a painful experience.

It can be a challenging situation when we long for understanding and healing from someone close to us, like a husband, but they struggle to grasp or provide the support we need. While ultimate healing may be associated with Jesus for some, seeking empathy and understanding from loved ones is a natural human desire.

When our loved ones can't fully comprehend our struggles, it's essential to recognize that not everyone possesses the ability to navigate through their own challenges effectively, let alone offer guidance to others. Each person's journey is unique, and some may struggle to comprehend their own issues, making it difficult for them to assist others.

In your pursuit of being open, peaceful, and loving, you may encounter a truth that's both profound and challenging: people can only connect with you at a depth that reflects their own inner journey. No matter how much warmth and understanding you extend, no matter how many times you offer forgiveness even with no apologies, their capacity to truly understand and connect with you will be limited by their own self-awareness and emotional depth.

When you express your feelings to someone and they respond defensively or dismissively, it can be disheartening. In my situations, I came to understand it's entirely reasonable to distance yourself from the conversations. It's important to be heard and acknowledged in any relationship, and if that's not happening, it may be necessary to reevaluate the dynamic.

Just like a mirror, others can only reflect what they have encountered within themselves. If they haven't delved into their own emotions, fears, and vulnerabilities, they may struggle to comprehend the depth of yours.

It's important to recognize that this limitation isn't a reflection of your wounds, openness, or authenticity, but rather an aspect of human nature. Each person's emotional landscape is unique, shaped by their experiences, upbringing, and willingness to explore their own framework. While it can be disheartening when you long for deeper connections, understanding this reality can help you approach relationships with empathy and patience.

While I yearned for empathy from the person I sought forgiveness from, I reminded myself that Jesus' understanding and love were so boundless. His grace extended to me, offering a place of refuge for when I was hurting and weary.

This journey of seeking spiritual wisdom allowed me to grow emotionally and spiritually, helping me navigate moments of dishonor and disrespect with resilience and a renewed sense of inner peace. As I journeyed through the depths of my childhood trauma, I recognized the profound impact it had on my life. It had shaped my perceptions, affected my relationships, and hindered my ability to fully embrace joy and love in this now very complicated marriage. I began to unravel the tangled threads of my past. I overcame my emotions by understanding that the original trauma wasn't caused by him, but his lack of understanding still hurt.

I confronted the layers of pain and trauma that had resurfaced. Despite my efforts we had many irreconcilable differences, differences in belief systems and the character of God's word, differences in standards and principles and it became very clear that the journey towards healing would probably require paths that diverged.

At some point, I started to find myself in a constant state of self-examination, grappling with the perplexing notion of my own self-worth. It seemed as if every decision I made, every achievement I accomplished, and every mistake I committed during this time became fuel for this relentless inner scrutiny.

I believe the condemnation I felt and experienced came from the enemy, not my husband. Past experiences, critical remarks from others, and societal expectations had all contributed to shaping my perception of myself. The more I analyzed my actions and questioned my abilities, the more I felt lost and uncertain about who I truly was.

It wasn't an easy process, as it required me to confront my deepest fears and vulnerabilities. However, with time and self-compassion, I started to untangle the complex web of thoughts and emotions that had ensnared my sense of worth.

I began to also learn the importance of recognizing my strengths and achievements. Celebrating even the smallest victories helped me cultivate a more positive outlook on myself. I discovered the significance of surrounding myself with supportive and understanding individuals who valued me for who I truly was.

There may still be moments of self-doubt along the way. However, by continually practicing self-awareness, self-acceptance, and self-love, I began to slowly reclaim a sense of worth that was not dependent on external validations but rather rooted in my intrinsic value as a unique individual.

This marriage helped me realize newfound boundaries, and I learned to navigate the demands of stretching myself beyond my capabilities to accommodate expectations and please others. As I encountered overwhelming and unrealistic demands, the recognition of my limits became evident. This realization brought understanding and the significance of saying no when tasks exceed our capacities. It had led to burnout, neglecting my personal needs, and my sacred time with God. Embracing the ability to say no in a relationship context is not a sign of weakness but a sign of a growing self-respect and worth.

We may encounter situations where our boundaries are tested. Whether it involves saying no to activities that make us uncomfortable or standing firm in our decisions or beliefs. When faced with pressure from others, these moments of asserting ourselves can be transformative. By learning to say no, we should be able to foster healthy safe relationships and create an environment that respects our individuality and values.

These experiences that introduce us to new boundaries are invaluable opportunities. Embracing these lessons empowered me to navigate life with authenticity, resilience, and a deep sense of personal empowerment.

In my early years and after my trauma, I often struggled with feelings of inadequacy and insecurity, seeking external validation to feel accepted and valued. I had become a people pleaser. However, as I delved deeper into my faith, I discovered the profound truth that God had fearfully and wonderfully made me in His image. His Word reminded me that I am loved beyond measure and that my worth is not determined by the opinions of others, but by the One who created me and despite losing my temper, cursing, or wanting respect, God had even loved me on my worst day.

Accepting this truth didn't come easy. It took time and effort to unlearn the negative thought patterns and self-doubt that had taken root within me. I began to engage in self-compassion and embrace my imperfections, knowing that I am a work in progress and that it's okay to make mistakes.

To my surprise, in other relationships the more I encouraged others, the more encouragement I received in return. As I showed compassion, I found that same compassion returned to me when I needed it most.

This beautiful cycle of giving and receiving not only deepened my connections with people but also brought a profound sense of fulfillment and joy. I learned that by focusing on uplifting others, I could create a positive and uplifting atmosphere that enriched both my life and the lives of those I touched.

During this time, through one of our many conversations, he admitted that our marriage was not based on love, and he felt that his heart was never truly in it. Instead, he had entered into the commitment out of a sense of duty, trying to lay down his life and obey what he thought he heard God say and for ministry purposes only, while fervently praying for a new heart that could genuinely love me.

In the midst of this conversation, he candidly revealed his belief that both of us had married for the sake of the ministry. However, I couldn't help but interject, asserting that it was I who, in my moments of vulnerability, had bravely expressed my deepened emotions. Our exchange brought to light the complexity of our relationships and the various perspectives we held on the reasons behind our union.

It was a painful revelation that left me grappling with the complications of our relationship and the path forward. In the depths of my prayers, I found myself earnestly questioning God about the reasons to stay in a marriage lacking biblical love, emotional support, and compassion, especially as I was on a journey of healing from trauma. I grappled with the uncertainty of my emotions and wondered if I would always feel this way.

As I sought divine guidance, I couldn't help but question the purpose of remaining in a relationship that didn't fulfill the basic needs of love and support. I understood that healing from trauma was a process, and it didn't mean that I would be stuck in that state forever. Yet, I couldn't ignore the profound impact of my partner's actions or lack thereof on my well-being.

The idea of staying with someone who wouldn't provide and protect weighed heavily on my heart. I longed for the safety and security that a loving and caring partner should offer, but it seemed elusive in my current situation.

Prayer is about faith. It's why we're called believers, not beggars.

When a door closes, I always find myself knocking on it a few times. But if it still doesn't open, I have learned that I should let it stay closed. In career, in life, and in love. When you see the period at the end of the sentence, we need to remember to not try to turn it into a comma.

I suppose we need to know when something is over and move on. But I continued to want to understand, asking questions. Our conversations never seemed to involve compromise or understanding; instead, they often escalated into heated exchanges filled with blame. It's possible that both of us were consumed by pride, making it difficult to find common ground or empathize with each other's perspectives.

Even though I continued to offer counseling options, whether secularly or with our pastor, my husband remained unconvinced about its potential to help. We discussed the benefits of seeking professional support, but he couldn't see how it would make a difference in our situation.

After discovering that he had offered to pay his ex's gas bill, I felt deeply uneasy and concerned about his financial boundaries in our marriage. I decided it was best to have an open conversation with him about my feelings and the importance of managing our finances responsibly. He again saw no reason for me to be upset. As a result, I asked him to leave so that he could reflect on his actions and reconsider his priorities. Setting clear boundaries is crucial in any relationship, and addressing financial concerns is no exception.

During our conversations, it became evident that he consistently refused to acknowledge any fault or mistake on his part. Regardless of the situation or issue at hand, he seemed unwilling to accept responsibility or consider the possibility of the hurt I felt or the possibility of him being wrong. This pattern of behavior made it difficult to address and resolve conflicts constructively.

I heard God say, "Stop trying to get out of the mess the same way you got in it."

Proverbs 26:11 provides a fitting scripture related to the idea of trying to get out of a mess the same way in which it was entered:

"As a dog returns to its vomit, fools repeat their folly."

This proverb emphasizes the foolishness of repeating the same mistakes, likening it to a dog going back to its own vomit. It serves as a reminder to break free from that cycle and to seek wisdom in handling challenges.

Instead of resorting to the same ineffective methods, one should strive for growth, understanding, and a renewed approach to overcome difficulties through Jesus.

I realized that staying in a marriage solely because of external expectations of its potential, the fear of judgment, or fear of change would not lead to happiness or the fulfillment of my call.

In my prayers, I sought clarity and the strength to confront these difficult questions. I knew that God's wisdom would guide me towards the right path. But I questioned my discernment in what I thought God had ordained.

There was a profound sense of grace in time with the decision to separate and ultimately divorce, because without this marriage I would have never healed from that childhood wound.

I would have never understood boundaries and I would not have known my worth. I recognized that sometimes, despite our best intentions, two souls cannot fully heal in the context of a shared journey.

Divorce can be an emotionally challenging experience, and the lack of contact with my ex-husband only intensified those feelings, I suppose. I haven't had contact with him since our hearing.

Sometimes, accepting that there's no solution to change their feelings can be difficult.

For weeks I felt broken. In this world, often people believe that which is broken is without value. We generally try to avoid conditions of brokenness with our finances, our emotions, and our relationships with others. But carefully note this about God's kingdom, there is a large contrast here between the will of God and the will of man. The world despises broken people, but God takes pleasure in using broken things. In fact, God demands that we be broken before He can even begin to use us. Unless we throw ourselves at the foot of the cross, someday we will be condemned for our sins. We must come to the end of ourselves to come to Christ.

We must be broken if we are going to be usable. Brokenness brings you closer to God. He is repulsed by pride but impressed by and attracted to brokenness. The one thing He tells us He looks for in mankind is a crushed spirit. Brokenness begins to make us useful to God.

A person who is not broken is a danger to himself and to God's people, because he is self-satisfied, confident, certain of his ways, and unwilling to admit his dependence upon God. God resists the proud but draws near to the broken-hearted. A person who is wrapped up in self does not feel the need to stop and listen to God. This person already has it all figured out. The person who is broken is more likely to spend time listening to God.

In a crisis, all of those Christian clichés suddenly come to life. When the events of tomorrow are really uncertain, the sovereignty of God takes on a whole new meaning. God suddenly has to be in control. Romans 8:28 is always in the Bible, yet when the floor falls out from beneath us, this truth suddenly takes on a deeper meaning of truth and all things must work together for good.

The emphatic statement that all things work together for good does not mean that all things are good, however. It means that God is able to take all things and weave them together in such a way that the end result is good. Though this path may not be pleasant, He assures us that we will come to a point where we realize He has been in control every step of the way. We veer off course when we try to take over, so God brings along crushing circumstances that cause us to look to Him.

We read that Paul was constantly brought to the brink of desperation because God didn't want him to trust in himself. The closer you get to God, the more responsibility you are given by God, and the more you will be forced to depend on God. The ultimate requirement for every believer, every priest, every royal son and daughter of God is to fully and totally remain a child of God. There are many examples of men and women in the Bible who experienced times of deep despair while serving God faithfully. The greatest benefit of being broken is that it makes us more like Jesus. There is no better example of brokenness than the very Son of God on the cross, in the garden, betrayed, beaten, bloodied, and brutally treated by the men He created. When we are broken, we are exhibiting a manifest token of His suffering.

When we are broken, that is when, without fail, he brings us to breakthrough!

Experiencing a revelation about free will was a profound moment in my life. I came to understand that, just like God who will never cross our will and force us to choose Him, I could not make my husband love me, understand my pain, or want our marriage.

This realization was both liberating and humbling. It reminded me that as individuals, we possess the gift of free will, allowing us to make our own choices and decisions. God respects our autonomy, granting us the freedom to believe or not, to love or not. Similarly, I couldn't impose my desires on someone else, even if it broke my heart.

Accepting this truth was challenging, as it meant acknowledging the limits of my control over another person's feelings and emotions. Love is a complex and delicate aspect of life, and I embraced the idea that relationships should be built on mutual love and respect.

While it's natural to desire a loving and fulfilling partnership, I now understand that my happiness and worth are not solely tied to someone else's actions or feelings.

Genuine love is something many people seek, and it's perfectly okay to desire and require it in a relationship. Remember, healthy relationships are built on trust, understanding, and sincerity.

In regard to the Bible, it offered me guidance on how love should be expressed within covenant relationships.

Proverbs 31 is often regarded as a guiding passage for women, illustrating the attributes of an ideal wife. I read this chapter multiple times over the years. It describes a woman who is strong, diligent, and wise in her actions. And striving to embody these qualities led to personal growth.

However, I forgot that it's essential to remember that although the Proverbs 31 passage should be seen as an inspiration for women to develop their strengths and talents, it doesn't imply that a husband should be any less supportive, caring, or responsible in the relationship. True partnership and love are built on mutual appreciation and encouragement of each other's unique qualities and aspirations.

In making the decision to divorce, I recognized that the relationship didn't align with these biblical principles of love and respect. I had to prioritize my well-being. Taking care of yourself emotionally and spiritually is crucial on the path to finding a fulfilling and loving partnership.

In the process of forgiveness I realized it was an act of freeing myself from the burden of holding onto anger and resentment towards someone who had hurt me. It's important to understand that forgiving someone doesn't necessarily mean granting them access to your life or allowing them to continue their hurtful behavior.

Forgiveness is a powerful tool for personal healing and growth. It enables you to release negative emotions, promoting emotional well-being and reducing stress. However, it doesn't require you to forget or ignore the pain.

Forgiveness doesn't equate to reconciliation either. Rebuilding trust and restoring a relationship with someone who has hurt you requires genuine remorse, accountability, and consistent efforts to change their hurtful behavior. If these conditions are not met, it's perfectly acceptable to keep distance from the person, even after forgiving them.

Remember, forgiving someone is a personal choice, and it's okay to take your time to process your feelings. Prioritizing your well-being and making decisions that protect your peace and happiness are essential aspects of the forgiveness journey.

It's not uncommon to question your discernment and decisions during times of heartache. But it's essential to be gentle with yourself and understand that feelings and relationships can change over time. Love doesn't always follow a straightforward path, and sometimes we find ourselves drawn to people who may not be the best match for us.

I've learned that it's important to recognize that human emotions and divine guidance can sometimes intertwine in complex ways. While it's natural to seek answers and validation from God, understanding and accepting your own emotions is a process that doesn't always have clear-cut answers.

I've learned to reflect on the lessons I've learned from this experience...

Through the pain of divorce, I found understanding that sometimes grace lies in letting go, in acknowledging the need for individual healing and growth and that we should never look at someone's potential—we should look at their actions. I held onto the belief that God's love and grace could bring restoration and renewed purpose, even in the face of shattered dreams.

Reflecting on the situation, I couldn't help but question why I hadn't examined the underlying issues beforehand. Perhaps the fast-paced nature of modern life had clouded my judgment and, in the hastiness, I had forgotten that God is patient and works according to His divine plan, while the enemy is impulsive, quick to make decisions. and he seeks only to disrupt God's intentions.

Maybe I was afraid to confront the realities that lay beneath the surface of my relationship and how quickly he wanted to get married. Maybe I looked past all the warnings and I hadn't listened to the insight of those who told me to take it slow. Maybe I thought that I could push him into his own calling. Maybe I just so desperately wanted a plus one to further the kingdom.

Regardless of the reasons, I realized that quick decisions can lead us down unexpected paths. I learned that God was always urging me to pause and seek deeper understanding before taking major life steps.

Through my spiritual journey, I've learned that God's grace is not about perfection or avoiding difficult situations. Instead, it's a compassionate embrace that carries us through the darkest times, offering hope and a chance for growth. I discovered that looking inward with honesty and courage allowed me to confront my mistakes and shortcomings. Embracing vulnerability and seeking forgiveness, both from God, others, and myself. It has been an essential part of another one of my healing processes.

While I can't change the past, I can use this experience as a steppingstone for personal growth and a deeper connection with God's loving presence. As I move forward, I strive to make decisions with greater mindfulness, seeking divine guidance and wisdom to lead me on a path of true fulfillment and inner peace.

I am sincerely grateful for my ex-husband's role in exposing my childhood wound and my lack of self-worth. It has allowed me to confront and heal from it.

Though our path together has ended, I have found the capacity to forgive, knowing that as imperfect beings, we all make mistakes. Despite the challenges we endured during our time together, I choose to release any lingering resentment, liberating myself from the weight of negativity. My fervent prayers are directed towards his journey of healing, for I believe that he possesses numerous admirable qualities that deserve recognition.

Throughout our time together, I witnessed firsthand some of his kindness whether genuine or not. However, like all of us, I undoubtedly know he also carried his own struggles and emotional wounds. It is my hope that he confronts those internal battles with unwavering courage, transcending obstacles that might continue to hinder his personal growth and happiness.

I envision him embracing life's invaluable lessons, extracting wisdom from past experiences, and gradually evolving into someone who confidently walks the path of his true calling, adorned with grace and purpose. But to do so, he must face his inner struggles with compassion and resolve, discovering the profound strength and resilience that lies within him.

I pray that the guiding light of the Lord leads him towards self-awareness and emotional growth, illuminating the areas in his heart that could benefit from tenderness and understanding. May he find the support of loved ones, who provide the encouragement and care needed during trying times without enabling him to remain stuck.

In the process of healing, I hope he learns to extend the same forgiveness and understanding to himself that I now extend to him. Through this act of self-compassion, he can unshackle himself from the burdens of the past.

In faith I believe he will find fulfillment in his endeavors, experiencing the joy that emanates from living an authentic life, As he traverses his own transformative journey, may the benevolent blessings of the Lord accompany him every step of the way.

I am going to share some ways I learned to forgive. Forgiveness is always a process as new hurts occur or are remembered:

1. Acknowledge your feelings:

It's essential to recognize and accept the emotions you experienced during that time. Allow yourself to process and understand them without judgment.

2. Understand the impact:

Reflect on how the events affected you emotionally, mentally, and physically. Recognizing the impact can provide insight into why you might be finding it difficult to forgive.

3. Empathize with yourself and the other person:

Try to understand the circumstances and perspectives of both yourself and the person you want to forgive. Empathy can create a pathway to forgiveness.

4. Set boundaries:

Establish healthy boundaries to protect yourself from similar hurtful experiences in the future. Boundaries are crucial for self-care and growth.

5. Practice self-compassion:

Be gentle with yourself throughout the forgiveness process. Accept that it's okay to have mixed feelings, and that healing takes time.

6. *Let go of resentment:*

Holding onto resentment can be detrimental to your well-being. Consider letting go of negative feelings to free yourself from emotional burdens.

7. *Seek support:*

Talking to a pastor, mentors, friends, family, or a therapist about your feelings and experiences can provide valuable support and guidance.

8. *Focus on personal growth:*

Use the experience as an opportunity for personal development and learning. Turn it into a steppingstone for positive change.

9. *Gradually forgive:*

Forgiveness is a process, and it's okay if it doesn't happen overnight. Be patient with yourself and allow forgiveness to unfold naturally.

Remember, forgiving someone doesn't mean you condone their actions; it's about releasing yourself from the weight of resentment and finding peace within.

As time passed, through this process, I began to rediscover my own strength, resilience, and capacity for love. I learned how to set boundaries and know when to say no. This was a challenge because throughout my life "no" was never a part of my vocabulary. But as I learned, I realized it aligned with every Christian principle and teaching. In Genesis, God established boundaries when He created the world and set certain limits in place. As humans, we can learn from this and understand the importance of respecting our own boundaries and those of others.

The Bible also emphasizes the value of self-discipline and prioritizing what is essential. In doing so, we can better serve God, ourselves, and others with a clear sense of purpose and direction. Therefore, setting healthy boundaries can be seen as a way to honor God's design and maintain a balanced and righteous life. I found more understanding in knowing that my journey towards healing and wholeness was not dependent on external circumstances or relationships. Rather, it was an internal journey, rooted in the unwavering love and grace of God. A place I had forgotten and already traveled.

In the wake of the divorce, Revolution Ministries remained a constant source of purpose for me. It became a space where my own pain and experiences could again be channeled into compassion for others. I recommitted myself to serving those in need, extending the love and grace that had carried me through my own trials. And the team of volunteers continued to support me throughout the process of separation and eventually my divorce. They did so with grace, and they truly showed me unconditional love.

It has always been my encounters with Jesus that I found healing, redemption, and a newfound sense of wholeness. In the depths of my pain, I always turned to Him, seeking peace, healing, and restoration. With His gentle touch and unfathomable grace, He always mends the broken pieces of my wounded heart. As with all things in my life there is always pain in your purpose, and purpose in your pain.

It's amazing that the wounds I bore sensitized me to the pain and struggles of those around me, instilling in me a deep sense of compassion and a new burning desire to alleviate suffering.

As a chaplain I studied the stages of grief. These stages include denial, anger, bargaining, depression, and acceptance. While these stages can be applicable to grieving individuals, it's important to note that grief is a complex and highly individualized process. Although it can be generalized to a physical death, it also can be found in the death of relationships. Not everyone will experience these stages or in a linear or predictable manner, and the intensity and duration of each stage can vary greatly. But I have learned grief is grief.

Indeed, some people come into our lives for a reason, a season, or a lifetime. Each person we encounter plays a distinct role in shaping our journey and understanding of the world.

I learned so many things during this period. At the root of my anger, I discovered the primal instinct of fight or flight, which is a natural response to stress and danger. In contrast to my now ex-husband, who tended to isolate himself during difficult times, I felt the strong urge to fight for our marriage, for respect, for dignity, and for biblical truths. This fundamental difference in coping mechanisms also created tension and contributed to the breakdown of our relationship. Despite my efforts to save our union, sometimes instinctive responses, different mindsets, and the inability to compromise lead us onto new and separate paths.

Some individuals appear in our lives for a specific reason, to teach us valuable lessons or to help us grow in some way. Their impact might be profound, even if their presence is temporary. Once their purpose is fulfilled, they might move on, and that's okay. We can cherish the lessons they imparted and be grateful for the experiences shared.

Then, there are those who arrive for a season, bringing joy, companionship, or support during certain phases of our lives. They might be close friends or acquaintances who leave lasting memories but eventually go their separate ways. While their time with us may be limited, the impact of their presence can be significant.

There are the individuals who are meant to stay with us for a lifetime. These are the people we build deep connections with, forming strong bonds of love, trust, and understanding. They become our pillars of support and the ones we can rely on through thick and thin.

Recognizing that some people are here for a reason, a season, or a lifetime can help us embrace the ebb and flow of relationships. It reminds us to cherish each connection, regardless of its duration, and to be open to the unique gifts that each person brings into our lives.

Lessons are always valuable because they provide opportunities for growth, learning from experiences, and gaining insights that can be applied to future situations. Whether the lessons come from successes or failures, they contribute to personal development and better decision-making. Embracing lessons with an open mind and willingness to adapt helps us become more resilient and wiser individuals.

It's liberating to let go of the pressure to be someone I am not and to embrace all aspects of who I am. On some days, I am amazed by my abilities, conquering challenges with unwavering determination. Other days, I may feel like a wreck, grappling with doubts and uncertainties. But through these ups and downs, I have learned to appreciate the beauty of being human. Each moment, whether triumphant or challenging, contributes to the intricate destiny of my life. Healing, I learned, also means taking an honest look at the role you play in your own suffering.

I've come to understand that authenticity is a powerful magnet that attracts genuine connections with others who belong in your life. By being myself, I invite people into my life who appreciate and accept me for who I am. I no longer need to hide behind a facade, and I find strength in vulnerability and openness.

This journey has taught me that true happiness lies in self-acceptance. It is not about conforming to societal expectations or seeking validation from others; instead, it's about embracing my unique self, quirks and all. When you become merely an option for someone, it can be disheartening because it means they may not prioritize you or choose you consistently. However, it's essential to remember that you deserve more than being considered casually. You are worthy of being someone's constant choice, someone who appreciates and values you unequivocally. Your worth should never be diminished by being just an option; you deserve genuine love and commitment. Always remember that and hold out for someone who sees your true value. God has played a significant role in shaping who you are, giving you unique traits, talents, and experiences. Embracing yourself as a creation of God allows you to acknowledge your inherent worth and purpose. While you may have certain challenges to overcome, remember that growth is a natural part of life.

So, I wholeheartedly celebrate the joy that comes from being real, unapologetically me, and embracing the ever-evolving nature of my existence. With every step on this remarkable journey, I continue to discover new facets of myself and appreciate the extraordinary adventure of life.

As I reflect on the journey behind me, I can't help but embrace the knowledge that lies ahead. With a heart full of determination and a spirit unyielding to the challenges that await, I am ready to face whatever complexities, trials, testimonies, and triumphs come my way. Each experience, no matter how daunting, I shall count as joy, for they are the building blocks of growth and wisdom. As I move on and forge ahead, I carry with me the strength of my past and the hope of a brighter future, ever embracing life's unpredictable but exhilarating dance.

The Pardon

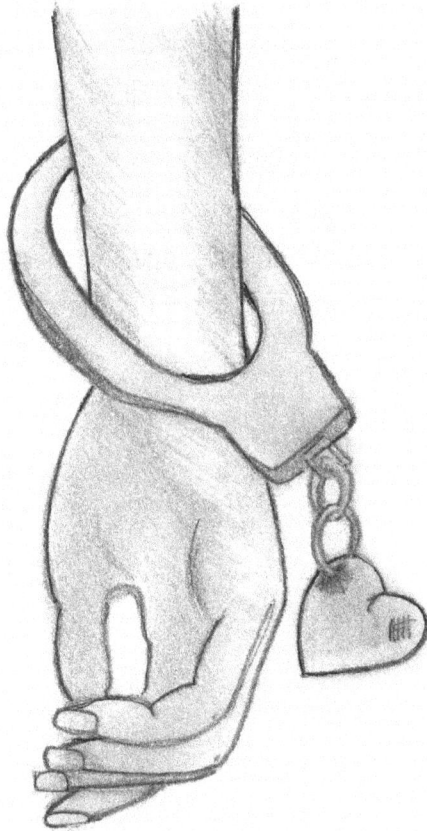

JML 20

My Gift from God "Nathaniel"

James 1:17

Every good thing given, and every perfect gift is from above, coming down from the Father of lights, with whom there is no variation or shifting shadow.

Amidst the trials and transformations of my life, there is a profound story of resilience, love, and the unbreakable bond between a mother and her son.

In the biblical context, Nathaniel is a significant figure mentioned in the New Testament. This is where my son's name came from. Nathaniel is often identified with the apostle Bartholomew, and his story is recounted in the Gospel of John 1:45-51.

According to the narrative, Nathanael was introduced to Jesus by Philip, another disciple. When Philip excitedly told Nathanael that they had found the Messiah, Nathanael was initially skeptical. He questioned if anything good could come from Nazareth, as it was not considered a prominent or highly regarded place.

However, when Nathanael met Jesus, something remarkable happened. Jesus immediately recognized him, even though they had not met before. Jesus said to Nathanael, "Here truly is an Israelite in whom there is no deceit." This statement surprised Nathanael because it seemed to indicate that Jesus knew something about him beyond what was visible on the surface.

In response, Nathanael asked Jesus, "How do you know me?" To which Jesus replied, "I saw you while you were still under the fig tree before Philip called you." This revelation deeply impressed Nathanael, as it confirmed to him that Jesus possessed supernatural knowledge.

Upon experiencing this encounter, Nathanael had a profound change of heart. He acknowledged Jesus as the Son of God and the King of Israel, expressing his belief in Jesus' divine nature.

The story of Nathanael illustrates the power of personal encounters with Jesus and the transformative effect of recognizing His divine identity. Though Nathanael's appearance in the Bible is relatively brief, his openness and honest search for the truth serve as an example for all who seek to understand and follow Jesus in their own lives.

It's fascinating to see similarities between my son, Nathaniel, and the character of Nathaniel in the Bible. In the Bible, Nathaniel is often depicted as a man of honesty, integrity, and genuine character. Similarly, my son exhibits these attributes. They are wonderful traits for him to possess. Nathaniel in the Bible was known for his sincerity and lack of deceit, as Jesus himself mentioned that there was no deceit in him.

As I observe my son, I notice qualities of openness, a willingness to seek the truth, and a genuine heart. These attributes can be a source of pride and comfort for me as a parent. Just like Nathaniel in the Bible, my son has become known for his honesty and authenticity, making a positive impact on the lives of those around him.

The name "Nathaniel" holds a special meaning in Hebrew, signifying "a gift from God." It is remarkable that this name carries such a significant message, as it reflects the belief that my son Nathaniel is considered a precious and divine blessing bestowed upon me and my family.

Just as Nathaniel in the biblical context encountered Jesus and found enlightenment, I Nathaniel has experienced the profound love and guidance of God in his own life.

Nathaniel has been a constant source of strength and support throughout my journey. From a young age, he witnessed the challenges and victories that shaped my life.

His belief in me became a constant source of motivation, pushing me to push myself further and believe in my own abilities. Through his encouragement and unwavering confidence, he instilled in me a deep sense of self-belief, transforming moments of doubt into opportunities for growth.

Nathaniel has always worked hard at school, excelling in his studies, and embracing every opportunity to learn and grow, though struggles not his own.

Through the journey of my own grief and the painful loss of Kenny, I found myself navigating through the darkness, desperately seeking some meaning. In those trying times, I struggled to recognize and acknowledge my son's grief, inadvertently failing as a mother to understand the depth of his emotions. Wrapped up in my own sorrow, I unintentionally neglected his pain, when he needed a mother's support the most.

As I gradually healed from the heartache, a newfound awareness dawned upon me. I realized the significance of making amends and asking my son for forgiveness, seeking that for the times I had unknowingly let him down. It must have been incredibly difficult for a sixteen-year-old to comprehend the complexities of his mother's grief while trying to overcome and navigate his own.

Let's not also forget the normal grappling that comes with the normal teenage challenges. But in his magnanimity, he forgave me, illustrating the resilience and maturity he possessed beyond his years. He is a wise soul.

During this profound healing process, I began noticing what I can only describe as "God winks" in his own life, meaningful coincidences that seemed to hold a divine touch. The first of these gentle nudges came when Nathaniel got his license and first license plate. To our astonishment it displayed the letters "JMK." A poignant reminder of Kenny's presence, these initials offered assurance that maybe although not scriptural Kenny was watching over us. Then, on Kenny's birthday, a day that held both joy and sorrow, my ex-husband's daughter was born, serving as a testament to life's interconnectedness and the beauty that can arise even amidst pain.

These God winks provided a sense of reassurance and hope, reminding me that love transcends the boundaries of time and space. They reaffirmed our experiences, guiding us through grief and healing. As I continue to navigate the complexities of life, I hold on to these precious signs, cherishing the journey of growth, forgiveness, and divine guidance that has brought my son closer to his own calling.

Throughout his life, my son has experienced a sometimes-wavering lack of substantial support and positive male role models. However, amidst this void, Kenny emerged, and he provided a decent foundation even through his struggling recovery.

As a mother deeply invested in my son's well-being, I sought to bridge the gap by offering unwavering encouragement and guidance. While my intentions were rooted in love and concern, it's possible that in my earnestness to compensate for the absent male figures, I may have inadvertently become overprotective. A helicopter mom if you will.

As my son and I have always communicated openly, it became evident that I had inadvertently sheltered him, hindering his ability to form many friendships at a young age. This was profound but something I could not fix. Finding the delicate balance between nurturing his growth and fostering independence is a natural challenge for any caring parent.

I've humbly realized that I can continue to be a pillar of support for my son while also allowing him the space to develop and discover his own path in life. Hopefully the combination of my caring presence and Kenny's positive influence and teaching of a relationship with God will help him navigate into his own personal growth and development.

Through the years, Nathaniel not only observed my life transform—my struggles, my triumphs, and the profound impact of Jesus' love in our lives but he also lived it. He witnessed rejection, the ways addiction hurts families. He saw how homelessness affected communities and the aftermath of death and divorce.

But he also witnessed love and faith in the family of believers that are in our life and reconciliation and restoration in family relationships. He has overcome adversities and witnessed the tangible love and benefits of being a believer of Jesus Christ. I hope he also got to see his role in which faith, compassion, and resilience shaped my path. He has had to embrace many lessons because of many of my wrong choices.

I remember seeing a picture once. In the picture, I saw a striking contrast between a homeless man and a well-dressed businessman. They were asked the same question: What had shaped their lives? Surprisingly, they both responded with the same poignant phrase, "My dad was an alcoholic."

Their answers revealed the profound impact of their upbringing on their current circumstances. Despite sharing similar pasts, their paths had diverged drastically.

The homeless man seemed worn and carried a burden of emotional scars from his upbringing. His experiences seemed to have taken a different toll on him, leading to a life of hidden struggles and coping mechanisms.

In contrast, the businessman appeared successful, with a spark of resilience, highlighting the human capacity to overcome adversity. He mentioned how he had endured hardships and tried to find strength in the face of challenges.

This left me contemplating the complexities of human existence. It became apparent that while circumstances can significantly influence one's journey, it is the individual's resilience and response to life's trials that can shape their outcome. Some find the strength to rise above their circumstance, while others may carry the weight of their experiences indefinitely.

It served as a stark reminder that everyone has a story, and we should approach each other with empathy and compassion, recognizing the potential for resilience or vulnerability in every person we encounter. The picture became a symbol of the human spirit's capacity to persevere, or falter, in the face of life's trials.

Nathaniel showed remarkable resilience at a young age. Even during my pregnancy, he faced numerous challenges, including my preterm labor and weekly doctor's appointments. When Nathaniel was born, there were moments of concern regarding his health and the possibility of heart issues. We endured a week-long stay in the hospital as new parents, grappling with the uncertainty of the situation.

Amidst all the trials, I held onto the belief that God was watching over Nathaniel with a protective hand. This knowledge gave me a profound sense of reassurance and peace, even in the midst of the uncertainties and scares we faced. It was as if I could feel His presence guiding us through the challenging moments, reminding me that there was a plan greater than my worries.

Trusting in God's protection, I found the strength to navigate each hurdle with a heart full of hope and gratitude. As Nathaniel grew, he encountered the challenges of being bullied at school and then the added burden of dealing with his stepdad's addiction. Despite the hardships, he remained determined and strong, never letting the negativity define him. Throughout the difficult times, Nathaniel's unwavering spirit and optimism kept him going.

Through bullying he confronted issues on the playground, without fighting or being mean. He showed authority, leadership skills and had empathy. He also befriended others who were bullied by helping them to navigate through challenges.

As he witnessed his stepdad struggle with addiction, Nathaniel chose forgiveness over resentment. He offered understanding and encouragement during the toughest moments. Nathaniel's journey taught him valuable life lessons. He learned to face adversity head-on. He always emerged stronger and exemplified the power of perseverance.

Nathaniel has shown an unyielding spirit that refuses to be defeated. He takes each hurt he has been through as an opportunity to learn and grow. Nathaniel's exposure to various experiences has likely shaped his perspective, and that might be why he hasn't rebelled in his young life. Understanding and seeing the consequences of drugs and bad choices may have helped him avoid heading down the wrong paths.

He remains undeterred, even when the road he's on seems daunting. It's not just about conquering difficulties for Nathaniel; it's about embracing them as a chance to develop into a better version of himself. He has never let obstacles define him. Instead, he has always harnessed them to fuel his motivation and propel him forward.

In the face of doubt and skepticism, Nathaniel stays true to his beliefs and values. Although sometimes very different from mine, I see him dedicated to his goals and I know he will work tirelessly to turn his dreams into reality.

Nathaniel is an integral part of the Revolution Ministries, lending his support, his muscles, his talents, and his compassionate heart to the cause. He is the backbone metaphorically and physically.

I'm not sure he truly grasps his innate understanding of his worth and calling, which is truly remarkable to witness.

From a very early age, Nathaniel's intelligence shone brightly, revealing a depth of understanding and a thirst for knowledge that was beyond his years. Whether it was exploring books, engaging in thought-provoking conversations with debate, or delving into various subjects, he showed a natural inclination towards learning and understanding the world around him.

Nathaniel is a fascinating young man, with a truly diverse range of interests that have shaped his life in unique ways. At the young age of sixteen, he embarked on a journey to obtain his ham radio license, showing a keen fascination for technology and communication.

Nathaniel's carefree spirit is seen in his taste in music. It is eclectic and eccentric. From Blink-182, and their catchy hooks and relatable lyrics to Journey, who has soaring guitar solos and powerful vocals. He can be found listening to my playlist which includes contemporary Christian which can infuse many spiritual themes.

Through his ongoing love for music, Nathaniel not only enjoys listening to his favorite bands but also dedicated time to learn the guitar and harmonica. His musical journey, I believe, became a creative outlet for him, allowing him to express himself.

His wide-ranging tastes in music serve as a bridge that connects him with a diverse community. By embracing various genres, he opens himself up to different cultures, experiences, and perspectives. When he interacts with others who share his passion for music, they can bond over their favorite artists, songs, and concerts. His openness to exploring different musical styles has brought a sense of inclusivity and understanding among people who might otherwise have little in common. He has definitely found common ground that builds relationships with individuals from all walks of life, ages, races, and belief systems.

He was always interested in the world of technology from a very young age, His intelligence baffles me. He has always been my go-to when I have been locked out of an account or erased something of meaning. I was excited when He decided to take cyber security his junior and senior years of high school.

In addition to these passions, he also has a profound interest in the history of buildings, roads, and towns. I often find him exploring the architectural marvels of the past. Understanding the evolution of towns throughout time excites him. From majestic castles to quaint villages, he has always immersed himself in the rich stories they hold. His desire to preserve and share these historical gems fuels his fascination, and he often takes joy in sharing his discoveries with others to inspire a deeper appreciation for the past.

Beyond his hobbies and interests, Nathaniel's character shines through in his role as a good friend. He values the importance of meaningful connections and goes the extra mile to be there for those he cares about. Whether it's offering a listening ear, providing a helping hand, or simply being a reliable presence, his friends know they can count on him.

Nathaniel's life journey is a testament to the power of curiosity and the willingness to embrace diverse interests. His insatiable thirst for knowledge and creativity has allowed him to flourish in various ways, bringing joy to those around him. As he continues to explore and learn, there's no doubt that Nathaniel's future holds even more exciting ventures and meaningful connections.

It's not just his intelligence that stands out to me or his hobbies and interests. It is how well he puts it all together. He possesses a balanced blend of analytical thinking and creative problem-solving, making him a well-rounded individual with an impressive skill set.

Throughout it all, it is evident that Nathaniel has so much worth and undoubtedly a higher calling. He seems to be in tune with most of his passions and talents. He carries himself with a sense of purpose and conviction, which is both inspiring and rare for someone of his age.

I deeply pray for my son to see himself in the same loving and compassionate light that God and others see him. I hope he recognizes his inherent worth, the unique talents he possesses, and the goodness he brings to the world. My prayer is for him to embrace his strengths, acknowledge his potential, and find confidence in his abilities. If I could show him how he is viewed through the eyes of love and acceptance, he might realize the positive impact he has on the lives of those around him. By understanding his true value, I believe he can develop a stronger connection to his purpose in life. I want Nathaniel to thrive with a genuine understanding of his own worth, just as others do, and find fulfillment in being his authentic self.

As a parent, witnessing Nathaniel's journey fills me with pride and awe. With God's guidance and his own unwavering spirit, there is no doubt that Nathaniel will continue to shine brightly, leaving a lasting positive influence on the world around him.

He is not only my son but also at times has been my confidante, someone I can be vulnerable and honest with. He is my sounding board, and like Jesus sometimes even my rock. He saved my life. There were many times I wanted to give up. But in his presence, I found joy, knowing that no matter the challenges I faced, he was there, standing by me.

Together, we celebrated the transformations and milestones of life—his ongoing accomplishments, my healing, and the growth we experienced as individuals and as a family. Nathaniel's own journey, although thrown into challenges, has proven one of faith and integrity, standards and principles this hurting world needs.

Nathaniel's presence in my life reminds me that transformation and healing extend beyond oneself—it ripples outward, touching the lives of those closest to us. His unwavering belief in me and the ministry fuels my determination to continue making a difference, knowing that people working together, young and old, are always going to be agents of change and compassion.

In Nathaniel's story, intertwined with mine, there lies a beautiful tapestry of love, growth, and the transformative power of faith. God knew exactly what I needed when he knitted him in my womb. We have continued to navigate life's twists and turns. I have faith that our bond and the love shared will carry us through every season. He will be eighteen soon and I pray that with each new season he remains steadfast, with the protection of God continually around him.

Since the time my son was in my womb, I have been faithfully praying heartfelt prayers over him. From the very beginning of his existence, I sought God's blessings, asking for protection, to make him intelligent, for him to walk in health, and happiness.

I prayed for my little one, even before his anticipated arrival. And as fate would have it, he was born three weeks early, entering this world with a sense of eagerness and anticipation. I couldn't help but notice the spark within him, showing glimpses of his future potential. Throughout his childhood, he continually surpassed milestones with ease, demonstrating an innate ability to face challenges head-on, metaphorically proving that he's always been ahead of the game.

Just as he arrived ahead of schedule into the world, he seemed to tackle life's obstacles with a similar zeal, always eager to explore and learn. His curiosity and quick understanding of things around him have been a constant source of contentment for me.

As he grew older, my prayers took on new significance, as I asked for God's guidance in preparing him to become a man of integrity and an asset to society. I prayed that the values imparted to him would be deeply ingrained, guiding him to make compassionate and responsible choices throughout his life.

With each passing day, my prayers for him have been filled with gratitude and hope, knowing that he carries an extraordinary spirit that will undoubtedly lead him. As he ventures further into adulthood, I remain steadfast in my prayers, confident that his journey will be marked by continued success. In every prayer, I trust that God's divine grace is watching over him, nurturing his growth, and guiding him.

In my heartfelt prayers for my beloved son's future, above all else, I earnestly seek God's blessings. I pray that he may always be in his presence and follow the will of God throughout his life's journey, walking a path of righteousness and guided by faith.

With eager expectations, I look forward to the future, wondering what God may have in store for this brilliant young man's life and call. I'm honored to call him my son! Maybe, just maybe, he'll even become the next president, ruling the country with his wit and charm or a lawyer because he carries traits such as being analytical, persuasive, and has the ability to argue effectively. Who knows? The possibilities are endless! But one thing's for sure, he'll always have my unwavering support and love, no matter where life takes him.

As a parent, I acknowledge that I may have fallen short at times, making mistakes along the journey of raising my son. There were moments of doubt, uncertainty, and moments where I wish I could have done better.

However, in the midst of those challenges, I also hold on to the hope that I did my best in most situations.

Parenting is a complex and constantly evolving role, and it doesn't come with a manual. I know there were times when my patience wore thin, or I made decisions that, in hindsight, might not have been the best. But amidst those moments, I also remember the times I hugged my son tightly when he needed comfort, listened attentively to his concerns, and celebrated his achievements with genuine pride.

I hope that the love and support I provided throughout the journey has left a positive impact on my son's life. I may not have been perfect, but I hope I have been a guiding presence, teaching important values, and instilling a sense of resilience and empathy in him.

Every parent faces challenges and acknowledging my imperfections doesn't diminish the efforts I put forth to nurture and care for him. My hope lies in the belief that my son knows I love him unconditionally, and that despite my occasional failings, I will always be there to support and uplift him in whatever he chooses to pursue.

I am positive I will continue to learn and grow as a parent, always being open to new approaches and understanding that mistakes are opportunities for growth. My love for Nathaniel remains unwavering, and I will do my best to continue to be the best parent I can. When the time is right a mother-in-law and grandmother as well.

As I age, I've come to recognize the significance of the proverbial cutting of the apron strings, allowing our children the space to chart their own course. It's a realization that our time with them is fleeting, a period in which we impart the values and principles that will shape their lives. God only allows a borrowing of them for a season. While our decisions may falter at times, the scriptural guidance from Proverbs 22:6 to "Train up a child in the way he should go, and when he is old, he will not depart from it" underscores our duty to guide their upbringing.

Oh, my heart, be still—the man my son has grown into fills me with pride. Even if he treads rebellious paths in the future, I'll forever stand as his mother. I pray our unbreakable connection will remain, and I promise I'll be his unwavering support, providing love, counsel, and assistance whenever he seeks it, as only a mother can.

As I write this, it is his last first day of school.

As I reflect on the pages of my life that I've chronicled in this book, I find myself lingering on this chapter. It seems that it remains unfinished, a chapter that revolves around the unwritten story of my son. It's as if the words I attempt to craft fall short of capturing the profound depth of emotion I hold for him.

In reflection maybe it is because he is one of the only people who has never broken my heart. Maybe because it is the closest thing to unconditional love I have ever felt or given.

Each attempt to convey his significance has felt inadequate, as if mere letters on a page. I struggled to encapsulate the immeasurable love and pride I feel. How do I transcribe the unspoken conversations, the shared laughter, the tears, and the silent support into a mere collection of sentences?

The weight of his importance in my life is beyond the ink's capacity, and so I find myself humbled by the challenge to capture his essence in words. This chapter, though feeling incomplete, is a testament to a relationship that defies linguistic boundaries—a relationship that speaks through the pauses between sentences and the unspoken truths.

The bond between a mother and a child.

My Gift from God " Nathaniel"

Similitude

Romans 4:16

Therefore it is of faith, that it might be by grace; to the end the promise might be sure to all the seed; not to that only which is of the law, but to that also which is of the faith of Abraham; who is the father of us all.

Throughout the seasons of my life, prayer and the diligent study of scriptures have been a guiding light, illuminating the lives of many Bible characters and their remarkable journeys of overcoming adversity. As I delved into their stories, I discovered more than just religious narratives; I unearthed profound lessons about life, resilience, and faith.

The lives of these biblical figures, though from a distant era, resonate deeply with my own experiences, struggles, and triumphs. Their unwavering trust in a divine God and then savior, their courage to face daunting challenges, inspired me to seek strength in my own journey.

I've come to realize that my spirituality isn't merely about adhering to rituals or following dogmas, but it's about cultivating a genuine and transformative relationship with the trinity. Through prayer, I find solace in sharing my deepest thoughts, fears, and hopes, knowing that there's an ever-listening ear.

The scriptures have become a wellspring of wisdom, a source of timeless truths that transcend the confines of any one person. I've learned that these ancient texts are like a mirror, reflecting the complexity of human nature and the beauty of the human spirit. As I read about the triumphs and tribulations of these Bible characters, I discover fragments of my own story interwoven with theirs.

In moments of doubt or despair, I turn to the lessons learned from the likes of David's courage in facing Goliath, Esther's bravery in saving her people, and Joseph's unwavering hope amidst betrayal. Their experiences encourage me to embrace life's challenges with fortitude, knowing that I, too, can overcome them.

This journey of spiritual growth has taught me that faith is not confined to the walls of a specific religious institution. Rather, it is an intimate connection with something beyond the material realm—a relationship with a divine presence that transcends understanding.

As the seasons change and life's chapters unfold, I cherish the invaluable insights gained from these biblical figures. Through prayer and scripture, I continually nurture this profound relationship, seeking guidance, finding solace, and growing in grace.

In the end, it is not about religious obligations or rigid rules, but about embracing the beauty of an ever-evolving relationship with our creator—a relationship that colors the canvas of my life with hope, love, and purpose.

Are there times I want to be mad at the things that have happened in my life? Like the prodigal Yes, but at who?

Are there times I want to ask why? Like Job, yes.

But God shared with me recently instead of asking why to begin seeking answers to questions like this:

W. H. Y?

What hurt me!

Who helped me?

Who healed me?

I am reminded of Kenny and how when I struggled with anything emotionally, physically, or spiritually he would say, "Lift your head, DEBORAH." He never programmed my name into his phone as Jody. He simply always had it as DEBORAH.

Looking back, I'm glad he spoke that over my life.

In all of my studies on Deborah I know she was a prominent figure in the Bible, known for her leadership and wisdom. She served as a judge and a prophetess during a crucial period in ancient Israel's history. Her story is found in the Book of Judges, where she is depicted as a woman of great courage and faith. She was known as a mother because she is mentioned as a mother of Israel. Her motherly role may symbolize her nurturing and protective leadership towards her people. But one of her most significant accomplishments was leading the Israelite army to victory against their oppressors, the Canaanites, under the command of Sisera. Deborah's unwavering faith in God and her ability to inspire and guide her people have made her a celebrated and inspirational figure throughout generations.

Deborah in the Bible doesn't ever question God's voice or wonder why. She didn't care about what others would say or think. She simply had the faith to do what God told her. She was a warrior, a fighter, and was willing to go into battle.

One of Kenny's texts to me said exactly this...

Feelings shift, Jody. Daily. Moment by moment.

But God's truth is immovable.

When everything we're going through—pain, loss, tragedy, grief—suggests that God can't help us or doesn't care, or it seems unwise to place our confidence in Him, NOTHING could be farther from the truth.

In the tumultuous journey of life, our emotions can often act as powerful forces, attempting to wreak havoc on our inner peace and stability.

They can lead us astray, clouding our judgment, and causing us to make impulsive decisions. Yet, amidst this storm of feelings, there lies a steadfast truth, an unyielding presence that remains unmoved—God's truth.

No matter how intense the emotional turmoil may be, the truth of our divine power's guidance and wisdom remains constant. It serves as an anchor in the face of adversity, reminding us that we are not alone in our struggles. While emotions may surge like waves, God's truth acts as a lighthouse, providing a guiding light to navigate through life's challenges.

By embracing and seeking alignment with this unwavering truth, we can find comfort and clarity amid the chaos of our emotions. It grants us the strength to resist being consumed by fleeting feelings, helping us make sound decisions based on principles that endure beyond the whims of the moment.

One scripture that speaks about having a sound mind is found in 2 Timothy 1:7: "For God has not given us a spirit of fear, but of power and of love and of a sound mind."

This verse reminds believers that God has equipped them with a sound mind, which is characterized by self-discipline, wisdom, and a soundness of judgment. It encourages them to rely on God's strength and love rather than succumbing to fear or their own emotions.

In times of distress, turning to this divine truth can offer us comfort and hope, reassuring us that we are part of a grander plan. It reminds us to have faith in the journey, even when our emotions try to steer us off course.

Remember, our emotions are an integral part of being human, but their intensity can be tempered by acknowledging the unshakable foundation of God's truth, allowing us to navigate life's challenges with grace and resilience.

In life, we have all faced situations that are completely unexpected and out of our control. These experiences are a great training ground to learn to depend on God, in all things. If we can learn to put our assurance in God, we can find that peace that transcends all understanding.

Healing, with Jesus by our side, can be likened to peeling the layers of an onion. Just as an onion has multiple layers that need to be gently removed, Jesus guides us through a gradual and patient process of uncovering and addressing various emotional, spiritual, and psychological layers.

At the core of an onion lies its essence, much like the core of our being where our deepest emotions and traumas reside. When we begin the healing journey with Jesus, we may start by addressing the outer layers—the surface-level wounds and recent hurts. With His love and grace, we gain insight into our immediate struggles and start to understand the impact of recent events on our emotions.

However, the true healing lies in going deeper, just as the most potent flavor of an onion is found at its core. As we continue to delve into our innermost feelings and long-buried traumas with Jesus by our side, we might encounter pain and discomfort, much like the pungent scent of the onion. This stage can be challenging and overwhelming, causing us to shed tears and confront our deepest fears. But with Jesus as our guide, we find comfort in His presence, knowing that we are not alone in our struggles.

With Jesus' love and compassion, we gradually reach the heart of our healing journey, where we find acceptance, forgiveness, and understanding. Like reaching the tender center of the onion, we discover our inner strength and resilience, knowing that Jesus is carrying us through every step of the process. Each layer we peel away brings us closer to our core, unearthing the wounds that have shaped us and allowing us to release the emotional weight we've been carrying.

The process of healing, with Jesus at our side, is not linear. It might require revisiting some layers or experiencing moments of discomfort. However, with His unwavering support and infinite patience, we continue to peel away the layers.

Ultimately, with Jesus' healing touch, as we reach the core of our healing journey, we find a renewed sense of self and a healthier emotional state. Like a peeled onion, we are now free of the layers that once held us back, able to embrace life with newfound authenticity and a lighter heart, all because of the love and grace of Jesus guiding us on this transformative journey.

As I continued to carry the torch of Revolution Ministries, I remained humbled by the knowledge that it was through my own healing that I had been called to serve. Each encounter, each life touched, became a testimony to the transformative power of Jesus' love for not only myself but all who believe.

With each act of compassion given to me, I seek to pay forward the immense gift of healing I have received. It was truly in the service of others that I found purpose, joy, and a profound sense of fulfillment. Through the ministry of Jesus, I am becoming a living testament, a walking epistle to the truth that brokenness can be transformed into strength and that healing is within reach for all who seek it.

I carry the scars of my own trauma, a visible reminder of the depths from which I have emerged. Beauty from ashes. And in every embrace, every word of encouragement, I whisper silent gratitude to Jesus, for it was through Him that I found healing, and it is through Him that I will continue my own healing and bring healing to others.

Through it all, Jesus is the foundation upon which Revolution Ministries was built. The cornerstone. His presence infused our actions, our words, and our very beings.

We trust in His divine guidance, knowing that as long as we remain faithful to His teachings, our efforts will continue to bear fruit.

And so, with Jesus as my guide, inspiration, and faithful team, Revolution Ministries will persevere. We continue to carry the light of His love into the darkest corners of society, offering support, and most importantly, a message of hope and redemption. As we walk in His footsteps, we will continue to witness lives transformed, hearts healed, and communities uplifted.

It is not just that the ministry thrives but our own spirits. We discovered the profound truth that in serving others, we are drawn closer to Jesus, and our faith blossoms with a deeper understanding of His boundless love.

With Jesus as our partner and guide, we continue to journey forward, dedicated to making a difference. It's his unwavering love, an enduring legacy that carries His message into the world.

God wants you to worship because it helps you focus on Him. God wants you to fellowship because it helps you face life's problems. God wants you to teach because it helps you fortify your faith. God wants you to serve because it helps you find your talents and gifts.

The women of the Bible exhibit incredible strength and perseverance, inspiring countless generations with their unwavering faith and determination. Take, for instance, the story of Esther, whose bravery and courage saved her people from destruction. Despite the risks, she fearlessly approached the king to plead for their lives, demonstrating her steadfast commitment to her community.

Another remarkable example is Ruth, who displayed unspeakable loyalty and endurance. Ruth, a Moabite woman, married one of the sons of Naomi, an Israelite woman. Sadly, both Naomi's husband and her two sons passed away, leaving her widowed along with her two daughters-in-law, Ruth and Orpah.

Despite the cultural differences and societal norms, Ruth chose to remain devoted to Naomi and her faith, refusing to leave her side. Her love and loyalty to her mother-in-law were truly remarkable. Ruth's famous words to Naomi, "Where you go, I will go, and where you stay, I will stay. Your people will be my people, and your God, my God," demonstrate her unwavering commitment.

As the story unfolds, Ruth gleans in the fields of Boaz, a wealthy relative of Naomi's late husband. Boaz noticed Ruth's dedication and kindness and was impressed by her character. Eventually, their paths crossed, and Boaz took an interest in Ruth. Their love affair bloomed, leading to their eventual marriage.

Now, because of Ruth's obedience and perseverance, she became one of the key figures in the genealogy of Jesus Christ. In the New Testament, the Gospel of Matthew includes Ruth in the genealogy of Jesus, tracing his lineage back through the generations. Ruth and Boaz became the great-grandparents of King David, making Ruth an ancestor of Jesus Christ.

The inclusion of Ruth in the genealogy of Jesus highlights the significance of her story and her role in the fulfillment of God's plan for the salvation of humanity and ultimately, the birth of Jesus. Her act of selflessness, love, and faithfulness continues to inspire me to this day. And it remains one of my favorite books of the Bible.

Then there is the story of Mary, the mother of Jesus. It is another powerful testament to perseverance. Enduring societal stigma and challenges, she embraced her divine calling with humility and strength. Her unwavering faith in God's plan allowed her to bear the weight of raising the Savior of the world.

Mary Magdalene was also a prominent figure and one of Jesus' closest followers. According to the New Testament, she was a woman who had been possessed by seven demons, and Jesus freed her from this affliction. If you remember In the first few chapters, I spoke about a childhood trauma. That trauma involved seven boys.

Experiencing trauma can have profound effects on you, leading you to seek ways to cope with the overwhelming emotions and pain. When I was victimized, it created a void within me, leaving me vulnerable and searching for relief. Unfortunately, I turned to rebellious behaviors like overeating, substance use, and engaging in promiscuity as a means to escape the distress caused by my traumatic experiences.

Rebellion, in this context, manifested as a way for me to gain control over my life or emotions, albeit momentarily. Overeating provided a sense of comfort, while substance use offered temporary relief from the emotional pain. Engaging in promiscuity was an attempt to find validation and connection amidst feelings of loneliness and vulnerability.

However, I'm grateful that the Lord eventually got hold of me, and it brought about positive changes in my life. Despite my past rebellion, I find comfort in knowing that most of it did not lead to long-term addictions or detrimental effects. This realization brings hope and strengthens my resolve to continue on a path of healing. Holding trauma inside and not discussing it or being vulnerable can be a challenging experience. Suppressing emotions and not sharing your struggles may have prevented me from processing the pain and finding healing.

By keeping it all within, I obviously inadvertently prolonged the impact of the trauma and my emotional well-being.

Talking about traumatic experiences and being vulnerable can be intimidating, but it's an essential step towards healing. Sharing your feelings with someone you trust can help you gain perspective, receive support, and start the process of healing. Remember, it's never too late to open up and seek help. I only realized this thirty-three years later.

Acknowledging your first mistake is a step towards growth and building resilience. Like Mary Magdalene, my journey shares elements of overcoming difficult experiences and finding redemption. Both our stories illustrate the power of finding hope and renewal through faith.

But just like Mary Magdalene I had a miraculous healing through Jesus. I overcame that trauma, and just like her I have become a devoted disciple of Jesus.

Mary Magdalene played a significant role in the events surrounding Jesus' crucifixion and resurrection. She was present at the crucifixion, witnessing his death on the cross. Later, she visited the tomb where Jesus was buried and discovered it empty, being one of the first witnesses to the resurrection.

According to the Gospel accounts, Jesus appeared to Mary Magdalene after his resurrection, making her the first person to see him alive again. This encounter is a powerful symbol of Jesus' compassion and love for all, regardless of their past.

Throughout the centuries, Mary Magdalene has been considered a symbol of repentance, faith, and the transformative power of Jesus' teachings. Her story remains an essential part of Christian tradition and has inspired countless believers around the world.

These women's stories are a source of inspiration, showing us that strength comes from resilience in the face of adversity. Their unwavering commitment to their beliefs and their determination to make a positive difference in the lives of others exemplify the kind of perseverance that can change the course of history. Their legacy continues to remind me that strength and perseverance can empower us to overcome any obstacles in our own journeys.

So you see I am a woman whose life was marked by trials, testimonies, and triumphant moments. My journey carried me through the depths of childhood trauma, the challenges of marriage, the heartache of loss, and the transformative power of faith.

Through it all, I discovered that there is purpose in pain, pain in your purpose, and that Jesus was working everything out for my good.

Although the wounds ran deep, shaping my perspective and leaving lasting scars, within the depths of my suffering, seeds of resilience and strength were planted. Little did I know that these seeds would bloom in the years to come, carrying me through the storms yet to be faced.

As I stepped into adulthood, I found love and embarked on the journey of marriage. But within the union, I encountered a different kind of trial—the battle against addiction. My spouse struggled with substance abuse, and my love was tested by the relentless grip of addiction. Yet, amidst the darkness, a flicker of hope remained. My faith in Jesus and my commitment to the power of love allowed me to stand by Kenny's side, supporting his recovery and believing in the possibility of redemption.

My journey took many unexpected turns when Kenny's life was tragically cut short plunging me into a sea of grief and sorrow. The pain was unimaginable, and the weight of loss threatened to consume me but even in the midst of my darkest hour, Jesus was there, offering solace and strength. His presence provided a glimmer of light amidst the shadows, and he carried me, reminding me that even in the face of death, there is hope.

Through my own healing and the ministry I co-founded, I chased the knowledge given by our savior and became a follower of his light making it a mission to share with others passing through this world, on their sick bed, trapped in poverty, homelessness, and addiction. My own experiences of trauma, becoming addiction's widow, and loss became testimonies of the resurrection power within us all, hoping to inspire others to find hope and healing in the midst of their own trials.

I believe Revolution Ministries became a platform for my compassion. Through it, I found fulfillment in extending love, care, empathy, and support to those in need. I realized that my pain had given me a very unique knowledge, allowing me to connect with others in a profound way. In my own brokenness, I found strength, purpose, and the ability to make a difference.

Through the ups and downs of my journey, I learned that Jesus took my trauma and turned it into a source of compassion. He took the struggles within my marriages and transformed them into opportunities for growth and forgiveness. He took the pain of loss and used it to ignite a passion in me for helping others. Jesus took the broken pieces of my life and crafted them into a beautiful mosaic, shining with hope, redemption, and purpose.

The female characters in the Bible have an enduring influence that transcends time and culture. These women's stories continue to inspire and empower women. Their strength in adversity, compassion in relationships, and leadership in challenging times serve as timeless examples for women to follow. The biblical women encourage women to break free from societal constraints, embrace their unique identities, and pursue their dreams with confidence.

Through their stories, these influential women continue to shape and enrich the lives of countless individuals, offering hope, guidance, and inspiration for women's journeys through life. Just like them through my story, I hope I can encourage others to find purpose in their pain, to trust in Jesus' faithfulness, and to embrace the transformative power of love and faith.

I know my redemption was only found in Jesus' love, and the profound truth that trials can be turned into triumphs. Messes become messages, tests become testimonies. In the hands of Jesus, pain can be transformed into purpose, and that through faith. Even the most devastating moments can be illuminated and used for his glory.

Healing truly begins when you can find gratitude even in your darkest moments.

Embracing gratitude allows you to shift your perspective, acknowledging that amidst the pain and struggles, there might be lessons, growth, and hidden blessings. It doesn't mean disregarding the difficulties you faced, but rather acknowledging them as part of your journey.

When you can be grateful for your worst day, you open yourself to the possibility of finding strength and resilience within yourself. It's a transformative process that empowers you to let go of bitterness and resentment, paving the way for healing and emotional release. By acknowledging the challenges you've faced and finding gratitude for the lessons they brought, you begin to cultivate a sense of inner peace and acceptance. My spiritual mom constantly reminds me that Jesus will love me on my worst day.

Being grateful for your worst day doesn't happen overnight, but it's a mindset worth nurturing. It allows you to move forward with a newfound sense of hope and a deeper appreciation for life's ups and downs. In this way, you can turn adversity into an opportunity for growth and self-discovery, ultimately leading to a more positive and fulfilling life journey.

I have beautifully drawn a parallel between my own experiences and the story of the woman at the well. Just like her and Mary Magdalene I have faced sin and darkness in my life, but I have also encountered the healing power of our king and savior.

The story of the woman at the well serves as a powerful reminder that no matter our past mistakes or struggles, Jesus meets us where we are with unconditional love and offers us the living water that quenches our spiritual thirst. Through His healing touch, we find forgiveness, redemption, and a renewed sense of purpose.

Like the woman at the well, your life may have encountered struggles, hardships, and moments of isolation. However, just as she experienced the transformative encounter with Jesus, you too can find solace and redemption through the grace of the Lord.

This divine grace has the power to cleanse, heal, and bring new meaning to your journey. It is a reminder that even in the midst of trials, there is hope, forgiveness, and the promise of a brighter future. Your connection to the woman at the well and the redemptive grace of the Lord reflects a profound understanding of the power of faith and the potential for personal transformation. May this awareness continue to guide and uplift you on your life's path.

Similitude

Legacy

Psalm 78:6

That the generation to come might know, even the children yet to be born, That they may arise and tell them to their children.

Your journey of healing and transformation holds the potential to inspire and bring hope to others who may be walking through similar struggles. By sharing the gospel and testifying to the work of Jesus in your life, you become a vessel of His love. The Bible says that you overcome by the blood of the lamb, and the word of your testimony.

In your vulnerability and transparency, you can create a safe space for others to acknowledge their own brokenness and discover the healing that is available through a personal relationship with Jesus. Your testimony becomes a radiant light, guiding others towards the freedom and restoration that can only be found in Him.

As you share your story, remember that the transformative power of Jesus is not limited by our past or the depths of our sin. He is a God of redemption, reconciliation, and restoration, capable of turning our brokenness into something beautiful.

I pray that your own testimony will lead people to the power of Jesus' love, the hope found in His resurrection, and the healing that comes through faith in Him. As you begin to share your own story, may others be touched by His grace and be drawn closer to the One who brings true wholeness and salvation.

Children of God, keep shining your light and sharing the gospel, for through you, lives can be forever changed. In your stories there are often elements of struggle and triumph, with characters facing challenges and enemies like the big bad Wolf.

But just like in those fairy tales, heroes and saviors can emerge to bring hope and save the day. Each person's life is unique and of its own, with its own plots, twists and turns, and sometimes unexpected heroes can arise to make a difference. What part of your story could help someone else? Is it the transformative work of Jesus, the hero rescuing you out of the darkness, the healing you received from the greatest physician of all times, or just falling in love with your King?

You play a vital role in spreading His love and bringing healing to a world in need.

The woman at the well encounters Jesus; a divine intervention becomes a transformative experience for her. I, just like her, recognize Jesus. I know He possesses something greater than the physical water from the well, he addresses her spiritual thirst and offers her a path to salvation.

This story teaches us several lessons. First, it highlights Jesus' love, compassion, and acceptance of all people, regardless of their background or societal standing. It reminds us that no one is beyond the reach of His grace and forgiveness.

Our own encounters with Jesus illustrate the transformative power of knowing Him personally. She leaves her water jar, a symbol of her old life, and goes to share the good news with others, becoming an evangelist in her community. Her story reminds us that encountering Jesus can lead to a change of heart, healing, forgiveness, and a desire to share His love.

The longest conversation Jesus had in the Bible was with the woman at the well. Their communication showcased the power of empathy, active listening, and meaningful dialogue, highlighting how effective communication can lead to healing and transformation.

I understand and appreciate the lessons and inspiration found in stories like these.

As their stories are passed down, they remind us of the importance of perseverance, compassion, and standing up for what is right. The lasting impression of these bible characters encourages and empowers current and future generations to embrace their own identities, overcome challenges, and forge their own remarkable legacies.

Living a life that leaves a lasting legacy is not only about making a positive impact on others and society but also aligning it with the teachings of the Bible and following the example of Jesus Christ. The Bible serves as a guide, offering valuable insights into living a purposeful and meaningful life. Jesus, in particular, exemplified love, compassion, and selflessness during His time on Earth.

As we strive to build a legacy, the importance of the Bible and Jesus becomes evident in several ways, and this is a list he has shown me:

1. *Foundation of Values:*

The Bible provides a solid foundation for ethical and moral values, which are essential in shaping our character and guiding our decisions. Jesus' teachings of love, forgiveness, and compassion serve as a model for how we should treat others.

2. *Servant Leadership:*

Jesus' life demonstrated servant leadership, where He humbly served others, putting their needs above His own. Following His example, we can lead with humility, empathy, and a desire to help and uplift others.

3. Impact on Others:

Jesus' ministry was centered on healing, reconciliation, and spreading the message of salvation. By emulating His approach, we can positively impact the lives of others, offering hope and comfort to those in need.

4. Eternal Perspective:

The Bible teaches us to focus on eternal values rather than temporary gains. By prioritizing spiritual growth and investing in the well-being of others, we can leave a lasting legacy that extends beyond our earthly existence.

5. Forgiveness and Reconciliation:

Jesus' ultimate act of sacrifice on the cross exemplified forgiveness and reconciliation. Embracing these principles allows us to mend broken relationships, promote harmony, and leave behind a legacy of unity.

6. Inspiration and Guidance:

The Bible contains stories of individuals who left enduring legacies through faithfulness and obedience to God. Their journeys inspire us to persevere, trust in divine guidance, and leave our mark in a manner that honors God.

Moses' calling was a generational calling. He wasn't just walking into something just for himself. He was fulfilling and walking into a covenant that was generational. It was the one God made with Abraham, Isaac, Jacob, and Joseph. It would then go to Joshua and so on and so forth.

Moses, a pivotal figure in religious history, experienced a profound and transformative call that transcended both his time and legacy. Moses encountered a burning bush, which spoke to him with the voice of God.

This divine encounter marked his calling to lead the Israelites out of Egypt and into the Promised Land. Moses' call went beyond him as his leadership played a crucial role in shaping the destiny of the Israelite nation, leaving an indelible mark on history. His teachings and the laws he received on Mount Sinai, such as the Ten Commandments, became foundational principles for ethical and moral conduct. Moses' legacy also extends far into the future, influencing countless generations with his courage, faith, and unwavering commitment to fulfilling his divine mission. His life serves as a timeless example of leadership, faith, and obedience to a higher calling that continues to inspire people from diverse cultures and backgrounds.

What God is calling you to goes way beyond and before you.

God intends on making you a part of his covenant. But it does not stop with you. We are called to be generational leaders.

Leaving a legacy through Jesus for the next generation with vulnerability and transparency is a powerful way to impact lives and share the essence of your faith. By openly sharing your struggles, doubts, and triumphs, you create an authentic connection with others, showing them that being a follower of Christ doesn't mean living a perfect life but rather embracing imperfections with His love and grace.

Through vulnerability, you allow others to see the transformative power of Jesus in your life, how He brings healing to brokenness, and how He guides you through the challenges of life. By being transparent about your journey, you provide a roadmap for others to navigate their own struggles, emphasizing that they are not alone in their experiences.

Your willingness to share both your successes and failures will help the next generation understand that faith is a dynamic process, full of growth and learning. It demonstrates that following Jesus is not about presenting a flawless image but rather embracing vulnerability as a means to deepen one's relationship with God and others.

In this way, you can inspire the next generation to embrace vulnerability and transparency in their own faith journey, fostering a community that supports and encourages one another. Through your example, they can witness the profound impact of living a life dedicated to Jesus, allowing your legacy to continue through generations, as they, too, choose to follow in His footsteps with openness, courage, and humility.

I want to be a leader in my community, just like my earthly father and my father God in heaven. I have always felt a deep calling to embark on a journey of pioneering, seeking to bring continued salvation to those who needed Jesus. As I step into my Christian role, my heart has always been filled with a sense of purpose and determination to spread the message of love, compassion, and redemption.

Setting out on this mission, I always felt connected with individuals who were also seeking spiritual guidance and support. Through heartfelt conversations and genuine empathy, I sought to understand their struggles and challenges. I realized that the path to salvation isn't always clear, and at times we all need reassurance, support, and a guiding hand that would continue to lead us to the light.

In my pioneering efforts, I helped my husband establish outreach programs and support networks that provided a safe space for people to express their doubts, fears, and hopes. These initiatives still aim to create a sense of belonging and foster a community of faith and understanding.

I am reminded of witnessing transformations in the lives of those I had the privilege to touch with the message of Jesus. I saw how the knowledge of Jesus' teachings would always be a catalyst for positive change and personal growth.

Challenges may have arisen, and doubts occasionally clouded my vision. However, the unwavering belief in the mission and the support of fellow believers still influences my determination to carry on.

Through this pioneering experience, I learned that being a leader wasn't just about guiding from the front; it was about serving, it was about walking alongside those in need, it was about sharing in their joys and sorrows, and offering hope in times of uncertainty.

As I continue to spread the message of Jesus, I must always remember to remain humble, knowing that the work is not mine alone. Together with Jesus and others who share the same passion, we will form a united force committed to bringing continued salvation to the lives of those seeking a divine purpose.

The rewards are immeasurable. Witnessing the transformation of lives and the healing power of faith has a profound experience that reaffirms my commitment to everything God has called me to.

It truly is not just a destination but an ongoing journey of love, forming a lasting legacy of hope.

In summary, building a legacy that aligns with the teachings of the Bible and follows the example of Jesus Christ brings deeper meaning and purpose to my actions. By living out the principles of love, compassion, and servitude, I pray I can positively impact others, leaving behind a legacy that reflects my own transformation, redemption through faith, and devotion to God's teachings.

Legacy

Triumphs

2 Corinthians 2:14

But thanks be to God, who in Christ always leads us in triumphal procession, and through us spreads the fragrance of the knowledge of him everywhere.

In the Bible, triumph is a recurring theme that represents the manifestation of God's power and faithfulness, leading to significant victories and deliverance for His people.

One of the most prominent examples of triumph in the Bible is the story of the Israelites' exodus from Egypt. After enduring generations of slavery, God raised up Moses as their leader to bring them out of bondage. Through a series of miraculous events and plagues, Pharaoh finally released the Israelites. As they reached the Red Sea with Pharaoh's army in pursuit, it seemed like all hope was lost.

However, God parted the waters, allowing the Israelites to cross on dry land. When Pharaoh's army pursued them into the parted sea, the waters returned and drowned the entire Egyptian army. This triumph signified God's power over oppressive forces and His faithful fulfillment of His promise to deliver His people.

In the Old Testament, the book of Joshua recounts the triumphant conquest of the Promised Land by the Israelites. After wandering in the wilderness for forty years, they finally entered the land flowing with milk and honey. Despite encountering fortified cities and powerful enemies, God led them to victory, securing the land promised to their ancestors Abraham, Isaac, and Jacob. This triumph showcased God's faithfulness and His commitment to fulfilling His covenant with the people of Israel.

Another significant biblical triumph is seen in the story of David and Goliath. The Philistine giant Goliath taunted the Israelite army, and no one dared to face him in combat. But David, a young shepherd boy, stepped forward in faith, armed with only a sling and a stone. He defeated Goliath with a single shot, symbolizing God's strength in the face of seemingly insurmountable odds. David's triumph demonstrated that God does not rely on human strength or worldly power, but He empowers those who trust in Him to overcome their adversaries.

The ultimate triumph in the Bible is found in the person of Jesus Christ. His sacrificial death and victorious resurrection conquered sin and death, providing eternal redemption for humanity. Palm Sunday, also known as the triumphal entry, marked Jesus' arrival in Jerusalem before His crucifixion. The people laid palm branches and their cloaks on the road, celebrating and proclaiming Him as the long-awaited Messiah. Despite His subsequent crucifixion, Jesus' resurrection on Easter Sunday stands as the ultimate triumph over death, sin, and the forces of darkness.

Throughout the Bible, triumph serves as a testament to God's sovereignty, His faithfulness to His promises, and His redemptive plan for humanity. It reminds believers that even in the midst of challenges and adversity, trusting in God can lead to extraordinary victories and deliverance.

In the midst of life's most profound challenges, finding healing and strength in one's faith can be a transformative experience. For me, the unwavering presence of Jesus during my journey through trauma, divorce, the loss of a baby, and then my husband has been a source of comfort. Through the depth of my struggles, I discovered that I was never alone, that there was a divine presence guiding me and leading me through my darkest moments.

In times of trauma, when emotional wounds seemed insurmountable, it was the boundless compassion of Jesus that embraced me, offering a glimmer of hope amid the pain. His teachings of love, forgiveness, and resilience became my guiding light, helping me find the courage to face the challenges head-on.

During the turmoil of two difficult divorces, Jesus stood as a pillar of support, reminding me of my inherent worth and strength. In the face of uncertainty, he reassured me that my value was not tied to my relationship status, but rather to the love and kindness I could share with not only others but also myself.

As a single mom, Jesus became the embodiment of the loving parent I needed, providing me with unwavering love, correction, and guidance. His example of nurturing and self-sacrifice inspired me to be the best mother I could be even in my many failures, instilling in my son the values of compassion, empathy, and resilience.

And in the final moments of my husband's life, Jesus offered his comforting presence once again, embracing me with divine grace and peace. As I faced the pain of loss, I found the promise of eternal life and the belief that my husband had found Jesus waiting for him at the entrance of eternity.

Through it all, my faith in Jesus became an anchor in the storm, grounding me in hope, and reminding me that with Christ I possess the strength to overcome life's trials. It was through this deep connection that I was healed, finding the courage to carry on and the capacity to love and cherish life again despite its many adversities. As I move forward, may the presence of Jesus continue to guide and uplift me and you, nurturing our spirit and empowering us to embrace the future with unwavering trust.

Life is a journey filled with challenges and choices, some of which may lead us down difficult paths. At times, we may make bad decisions that result in unfavorable consequences, but these moments also provide valuable lessons for personal growth. Throughout this journey, we must remain aware of the enemy of our soul, the negative forces that seek to undermine our well-being and happiness.

The challenges we face can be both external and internal, testing our strength and resilience. They can range from personal struggles like health issues or relationship conflicts to broader societal challenges that affect us all.

It is during these moments that our decisions play a crucial role in shaping our future. Some choices may bring success and happiness, while others can lead us astray.

Recognizing the enemy of our soul, often referred to as evil or negativity, is essential in navigating life's twists and turns. This adversary seeks to sow seeds of doubt, fear, and temptation in our minds, trying to divert us from our true purpose and potential. Being mindful of these malevolent schemes can help us guard against their influence and maintain our inner strength and peace.

As we encounter challenges and make choices, it's crucial to remember that no one is immune to mistakes. Embracing our imperfections and learning from our bad choices can foster personal growth and resilience. Moreover, understanding the strategies of the enemy of our soul empowers us to resist its allure and stay true to our values and beliefs.

In this journey of life, we must find strength in the face of challenges, wisdom in our choices, and the determination to withstand the schemes of the devil. By doing so, we can strive towards a more fulfilling and purposeful existence, fostering a sense of inner peace and contentment despite the difficulties we encounter.

In these difficult times, it is crucial not to forget the importance of going to war in the spirit—not a physical war, but a spiritual battle against the challenges we face. As we navigate through tough circumstances, prayer and seeking guidance are essential tools to find answers and strength.

Remember, our battles are not fought solely on the physical plane, but also in the realms of faith and perseverance. By staying connected to our spiritual selves, we can draw upon inner reserves of courage and hope to face the trials ahead.

Through prayer, we find understanding in a higher power, seeking comfort amidst uncertainty. It allows us to surrender our worries and fears, trusting that there is a plan beyond our own comprehension.

In seeking guidance, we turn to wise counsel, whether it be from trusted mentors, religious leaders, or our own introspection. It's essential to stay open to the lessons life presents and be willing to learn from them.

By combining the power of prayer and seeking guidance, we align ourselves with our true purpose and values, gaining clarity on the paths we must tread. In doing so, we can confront challenges with renewed determination, knowing that we are not alone. Let us never forget the significance of fortifying ourselves spiritually. By doing so, we equip ourselves to navigate the storms with resilience, finding the strength to overcome adversity and emerge stronger on the other side.

At some point in our lives, each of us requires support, guidance, or a helping hand. This realization should serve as a constant reminder to be kind, understanding, and supportive to those who may need assistance now or in the future. As we join together in supporting one another, we create a stronger and more resilient community, united by our shared faith and values.

In a world where it may seem overwhelming to feed the masses, we can find solace in the profound impact of helping just one person in need. Drawing inspiration from Jesus and his ministry, we realize that it is through individual acts of compassion and selflessness that true change often begins.

Jesus' legacy teaches us the value of leaving the comfort of the known (the ninety-nine) to seek out and uplift the one who is struggling. While feeding the masses may appear daunting, touching the life of one person can create a ripple effect of transformation that spreads far beyond our imagination.

By following in Jesus' footsteps, we learn to see the worth and dignity in each individual, and we understand that even the smallest acts of kindness can bring about profound change.

Whether it's offering a helping hand, lending a listening ear, or simply showing empathy and understanding, we can contribute to making the world a better place, one person at a time.

Let us remember that no act of kindness is too small, and each person we help is a step towards building a more compassionate and caring society, inspired by the timeless teachings of Jesus and his ministry.

Remembering that Jesus said to "love your neighbor as you love yourself" this ultimately means treating others with the same care, compassion, and kindness that you would want for yourself. It involves acknowledging the inherent worth and dignity of every individual and acting towards them with empathy, honor, and respect.

Loving yourself, in this context, means recognizing your own value and worth as a person. It involves taking care of your physical, emotional, and spiritual well-being, as well as forgiving yourself for mistakes and shortcomings. When you truly love yourself, you can extend that love to others, understanding that they too are deserving of love, understanding, and acceptance.

Those words emphasize the interconnectedness of all people and encourage us to treat others as we would want to be treated. By loving our neighbors as ourselves, we promote a world where empathy and love will always prevail, leading to a more harmonious and understanding society.

The human spirit is a remarkable force, capable of transcending adversity and discovering wisdom and strength in even the most unimaginable times. When faced with challenges and hardships, we often tap into our own resilience, courage, and inner fortitude to endure and emerge victorious.

These triumphs can remind me of archery because both involve skill, focus, and precision to hit the target successfully and achieve victory. Just like hitting the bullseye in archery, triumphing in any endeavor requires practice, determination, and accurate aim towards your goal.

Archery, with its concept of aiming and shooting arrows, serves as a profound metaphor for life's journey and the way setbacks can propel us towards our goals. When an archer draws back the bowstring, they encounter tension and resistance, similar to the challenges we face in life. These obstacles may seem daunting, but they are essential to create the potential energy needed for the arrow's flight.

Just like in life, setbacks and challenges can be disheartening, causing us to doubt our capabilities. However, when the archer releases the arrow, the potential energy is converted into kinetic energy, propelling the arrow forward. Similarly, when we face and overcome obstacles, we develop resilience, determination, and strength, which become the driving force towards our aspirations.

Every archer knows that hitting the target directly without any misses is rare. Likewise, in life, we may face failures and disappointments. But each miss offers an opportunity for growth and learning, allowing us to adjust our aim and improve our skills. The setbacks act as a feedback mechanism, guiding us on the path to success.

Additionally, archery teaches patience and discipline. In life, progress may not always be immediate, but with consistent effort and perseverance, we can inch closer to our goals. The process of aiming, adjusting, and releasing the arrow is akin to setting goals, adapting strategies, and finally achieving them.

Just as the archer refines their technique through continuous practice, we can overcome setbacks and challenges by refining our approach to life. Embracing failures as steppingstones and turning adversity into opportunity can lead us closer to the bullseye of our ambitions.

This metaphorical nature beautifully encapsulates the idea that setbacks and challenges are not roadblocks but catalysts that can propel us further towards our goals. By facing and conquering these hurdles, we become stronger, more skilled, and better equipped to hit the mark in life. It reminds us that success is not always about avoiding difficulties, but rather about embracing them as part of the journey and using them to our advantage.

The human spirit's resilience and strength have been witnessed in times of war, natural disasters, and personal trials. It is a testament to the depth of human potential when we put our faith in the almighty.

I want you to hold steadfast to the torch of faith burning within you. Like an arrow that is drawn back before it is launched forward, embrace the challenges and experiences that have shaped you, for they will propel you to be a guiding star, illuminating the world with the timeless message of Christ.

There will be times when you may feel uncertain or tested, just as an arrow experiences tension before soaring towards its target. In those moments, draw strength from the teachings of Christ, who showed us the importance of love, forgiveness, and compassion. Lean on prayer and the words of scripture to guide you through your challenges and decision-making.

Let your light shine brightly, not only in words but also in actions. Be a beacon of hope for those who may be struggling in darkness, offering a hand of support and a heart of understanding. Be a source of comfort for the brokenhearted and a champion for the marginalized and oppressed.

In a world often marred by division and conflict, let your faith be the unifying force that brings people together. Embrace diversity, respect differing beliefs, and foster an environment of inclusivity, mirroring Christ's message of love and acceptance.

Your mission is not just to be a passive witness, but to be actively engaged in making the world a better place. Show kindness to strangers, lend a listening ear to those in need, and extend a helping hand to the less fortunate.

In times of doubt, remember that Christ's love knows no bounds, and through faith, you can find the strength to persevere. Just as the arrow finds its mark through focus and determination, you too can achieve your goals with unwavering dedication to spreading the message of Christ.

Let your journey be marked by humility and a willingness to learn from others. As you touch lives, may the love and light of Christ emanate through your words and deeds, leaving a positive and lasting impact on everyone you encounter.

As I embarked on finishing this book, the third anniversary of Kenny's death eluded me. I couldn't help but feel the weight of emotions from the past. This month has always been tough, as it marks the finalization of my divorce, coinciding with the same day Kenny passed away. It's a haunting reminder of the painful sequence of events that unfolded in my life. Losing two husbands in different ways on the same day.

Throughout the month, there are multiple significant dates, each carrying its own bittersweet memories. Our wedding anniversary is a reminder of the love and joy we once shared, while his birthday brings back cherished moments we celebrated together. But it's also the anniversary of the loss of our baby, a heartbreaking event that forever changed me.

Romans 12:15: "Rejoice with those who rejoice; mourn with those who mourn."

The worst part of holding onto the memories is not the pain. It's the loneliness of it. Memories need to be shared, and I believe I have done that through these writings.

It's hard to believe it has been eleven years since I lost my baby. I suppose that it is impossible to go about life unchanged, when all we do, all our experiences, from the greatest to the insignificant, shape us.

Still… There are those things in our lives that leave a deeper mark upon us. Let's be honest. Healing is no easy task. Grieving, no simple one. One that took me much longer than I could have anticipated. My vacation to that beautiful chapel in the Smoky Mountains healed me in so many areas.

But even still… I have moments. Remnants of the raw ache that suddenly and unexpectedly courses through my veins bringing tears to my eyes. When I hold a beautiful baby and long to have held mine.

The feelings that hurt most, the emotions that sting most, are those that seem absurd—like the longing for impossible things, precisely because they are impossible; nostalgia for what never was; the desire for what could have been; regret.

Though July will always be permeated with heartache, I have Nathaniel and I am blessed to be a mother! I have restoration with my family, I have friends who love me, I have coworkers I cherish, I have a church who continues to support and encourage me, and most of all I have a God who knows my future!

Through it all I suppose God only wanted to remind me of His promises and His faithfulness amidst difficult and challenging times. That no matter how dark the landscape may seem to be, He will always be there for me and that all I need to do is call on Him.

In eleven years I realized, mourning can be a good thing. Loss always takes place for a reason; it hurts but it can be transformative if you embrace it. HE has promised to one day turn our mourning into joy.

And it makes me cherish those still here, it reminds me to say I love you more often, it reminds me to hug someone a little longer, it reminds me to take a breath and look at the beauty our God has created, it reminds me to cherish the little ones around me that will be grown in a blink of an eye, it reminds me to always give away what I want…the healing will come I promise you!

Against the grain, I find solace in the symbolism of numbers. I stated earlier the number seven signifies completion, a time to reflect on the past and find closure in the midst of trials. And as I walk into the month of August, I am reminded that the number eight signifies new beginnings, offering hope for the future and the promise of fresh opportunities.

I draw strength from my faith in Christ. Through Him, I find hope and the courage to face whatever challenges lie ahead. Despite the pain and loss of my past, I look forward to the new beginnings that await me, trusting that God has a plan and purpose for my life. It's in His love and grace that I find comfort and the strength to move forward, embracing the opportunities that are about to come my way.

On January 7th, 1977, I was born into this world, my own Genesis, and this date holds a special significance for me as well. As I journey through life, I carry with me the hope that when my time comes to return to glory, I will have accomplished and completed all that I was meant to achieve on this earthly plane.

Throughout my existence, I strive to use every opportunity, every talent, and every gift that God has bestowed upon me. I endeavor to live a purposeful life, leaving no potential untapped and no passion unexplored. With each step I take, I aspire to make a positive impact on the lives of others and contribute to the betterment of the world around me following in Jesus' footsteps and ministry to be his hands and feet with the bold empowerment of his Holy Spirit.

It is not about seeking praise or recognition from others but knowing that I have made the most of the life I have been blessed with and fulfilled the purpose for which I was created.

As I continue on this journey, I embrace both the triumphs and the challenges that come my way, for they are the building blocks of growth and transformation. I find unspeakable joy in the belief that the divine plan is greater than my understanding, and I trust that as I walk this path, I am guided by a higher purpose.

My triumphs do bring me unspeakable joy. Joy is a profound emotion that can be likened to an analogy of "Jesus, others, and then yourself." In this analogy, the order of priority signifies the essence of true joy. Putting Jesus first means finding joy in a higher purpose beyond ourselves, connecting with our faith, and seeking spiritual fulfillment.

The second part of the analogy, "others," highlights the joy that comes from selfless acts of kindness, empathy, and compassion towards those around us. When we invest in the happiness and well-being of others, we experience a deep and lasting joy that transcends personal gratification.

Finally, "yourself" reminds us that while it's essential to care for others, we must also acknowledge our own well-being and happiness. Embracing self-care, self-love, and pursuing personal growth can lead to a genuine sense of joy and contentment.

Ultimately, the joy that arises from this analogy stems from a harmonious balance of spiritual fulfillment, compassion for others, and a healthy appreciation for oneself. It's a reminder that joy is not merely a fleeting emotion but a profound state of being that encompasses our connection with the divine, our relationships with others, and our relationship with ourselves.

I look forward to the day when I return to the realm of eternity, knowing that I have lived a life of meaning, purpose, and love. I pray my journey will be filled with kindness, compassion, and selflessness, and that I leave a lasting legacy of positivity and inspiration for generations to come. And on that glorious day, when my time on this earth is completed, I pray that God will welcome me with open arms and say, "Well done, good and faithful servant. You used everything I gave you."

Triumphs

JML 23

Testimonies:
We All Have Faces

Revelation 12:11

*They triumphed over him by the blood of the Lamb and by the word
of their testimony; they did not love their lives so much as to shrink
from death.*

Throughout my journey, I have come to realize the profound truth that each individual carries their own unique narrative, a tale woven with moments of joy, sorrow, struggle, and triumph. It is a story that reflects the essence of our humanity and the universal thread that binds us all together.

In this world, we are no strangers to adversity or to each other and as we encounter the multifaceted facets of trauma, trials, testimonies, and triumphs. It is in navigating these arduous paths that we discover the beauty of resilience and the strength that lies within us. And yet, we are not alone on this journey. The ever-present grace of Jesus becomes our guiding light, leading us towards healing and restoration.

Embracing vulnerability and transparency, we allow ourselves to be seen and understood, not just by the divine but also by our fellow travelers on this road of life. Our willingness to open our hearts and share our struggles becomes a powerful testimony that transcends the boundaries of our individual existence. It becomes a healing balm for those who hear our story, reminding them that they too can find solace and hope in their darkest moments.

But there is more to this profound journey than self-discovery and personal healing. As we seek wholeness in our relationship with God, we embark on a transformational voyage. We become living epistles, walking testaments to the boundless grace and love of our Creator. Through our connection with the divine, we are empowered to rise above our limitations and embrace our truest selves, reflecting the image of love and compassion that is etched in our souls.

In this intertwining of personal healing and spiritual growth, we find a deeper purpose and meaning. Our actions, words, and deeds narrate a tale of hope and faith, a tale that resonates with the hearts of those who cross our paths. In our pursuit of wholeness, we not only mend our own brokenness but also offer the gift of healing to those we encounter, sparking a ripple effect of positive change in the world around us.

In life's intricacies, one truth remains unwavering: you are never alone in your struggles. Amidst the ebb and flow of existence, there are countless souls navigating their own trials, battling their own fears, and seeking their own contentment and peace.

Embracing traumas, trials, testimonies, and triumphs is a profound journey that shapes our lives and our character. Each aspect plays a crucial role in our growth and development, leaving an indelible mark on our experiences.

Traumas, although painful, can be transformative. By embracing them, we acknowledge the wounds we carry and begin the healing process. Confronting our traumas allows us to build resilience, develop empathy, and find strength in vulnerability.

Trials are an inevitable part of life, testing our perseverance and determination. Embracing these challenges enables us to learn valuable lessons, develop problem-solving skills, and discover our inner strength. Trials are opportunities for growth and self-discovery.

Testimonies are the stories of our experiences, sharing our journey with others. By embracing our testimonies, we find empowerment in vulnerability, knowing that our stories have the power to inspire, heal, and connect with others. Through sharing our testimonies, we build a sense of community and support.

Triumphs are the moments of victory, achievement, and celebration in our lives. Embracing triumphs allows us to acknowledge our hard work and perseverance, boosting our self-confidence and reinforcing our belief in our abilities. Celebrating our triumphs encourages us to keep striving for success.

Think of life as comparable to a glow stick. Much like how a glow stick needs to be shaken, cracked, and often broken in many places to release its vibrant light, life's trials and setbacks can shake us and break us at times. Yet, it's often through these very challenges that our inner strength, resilience, and potential illuminate the path ahead. Just as the glow stick's radiance is most noticeable in the dark, our ability to rise above difficulties and let our inner brilliance shine through the fractures of life's experiences can be our most inspiring and transformative moments.

In embracing all these aspects of life, we recognize the full spectrum of human experience. It is through the integration of our traumas, trials, testimonies, and triumphs that we find wholeness and authenticity. Embracing them all allows us to live life more fully, with compassion for ourselves and others. It is in these moments of embrace that we discover the beauty of our humanity.

In the following pages, you will find a collection of drawings that I have created during my journey through healing. While I may not consider myself an artist by any means, these pictures hold deep significance for me as they represent a significant part of my healing process.

Through the act of drawing, I found a way to be transparent and a way to express my emotions, thoughts, and experiences in my walk with Christ. Each stroke of the pencil became a form of introspection, allowing me to pour my heart and soul onto the paper.

In those moments of creation, I felt a profound connection with God, as if His guiding hand was moving through me.

These drawings capture various moments of my spiritual growth, from moments of doubt and struggle to times of profound faith and revelation. They are a visual testament to the transformative power of Christ's love and the healing it brought into my life.

As you thumb through the following pages, I hope you can feel the raw emotions behind each piece and experience the profound impact Christ has had in my life.

You will notice that faces in these drawings are left blank; this is twofold. Firstly, as I mentioned, my artistic skills may not encompass drawing intricate facial features accurately. But secondly, and perhaps more importantly, leaving the faces blank was a deliberate choice to encourage a deeper personal connection for anyone who ever viewed my artwork.

By omitting specific facial details, I intended to create a space for viewers to project their own emotions, experiences, and identity onto the characters within the drawings. We all have faces and each person who gazes upon these artworks can see themselves or someone they relate to in the blank faces, allowing them to form a unique and personal connection with the pieces.

It is my hope that these drawings transcend my own artistic limitations and become a mirror for others to reflect upon their own journey in Christ. Each viewer can see a part of themselves in these images, resonating with the themes of healing, faith, and spiritual growth.

May these illustrations not only inspire self-reflection but also serve as a reminder that we are all connected on our individual paths, seeking solace and healing in our own unique ways. And in the absence of detailed faces, may these drawings become a canvas for everyone to find their own reflection within the journey of faith and the transformative power of Christ's love.

"Every ending is a new beginning in disguise."

Transitions in life, although they may seem like the conclusion of something significant, are actually the starting points for new chapters. Change can be daunting, often bringing a mix of emotions such as uncertainty, nostalgia, and even fear. Yet, hidden within the closing of one chapter is the potential for growth, discovery, and fresh experiences. Just as the sun sets to give way to the night, it also rises to mark the dawn of a new day. When one door closes, another opens, presenting opportunities that may not have been evident before. I encourage you to embrace your change and view it as a chance to evolve, learn, and create new stories. It reminds me that even during times of endings, there's an undercurrent of hope and the promise of new beginnings waiting to unfold.

In closing, I want to express my heartfelt gratitude for the opportunity to share my personal stories. My traumas, trials, testimonies, and triumphs. May my openness inspire others to embrace their own journeys and find healing through sharing and the love of Jesus Christ.

Jody's Art Gallery of Healing

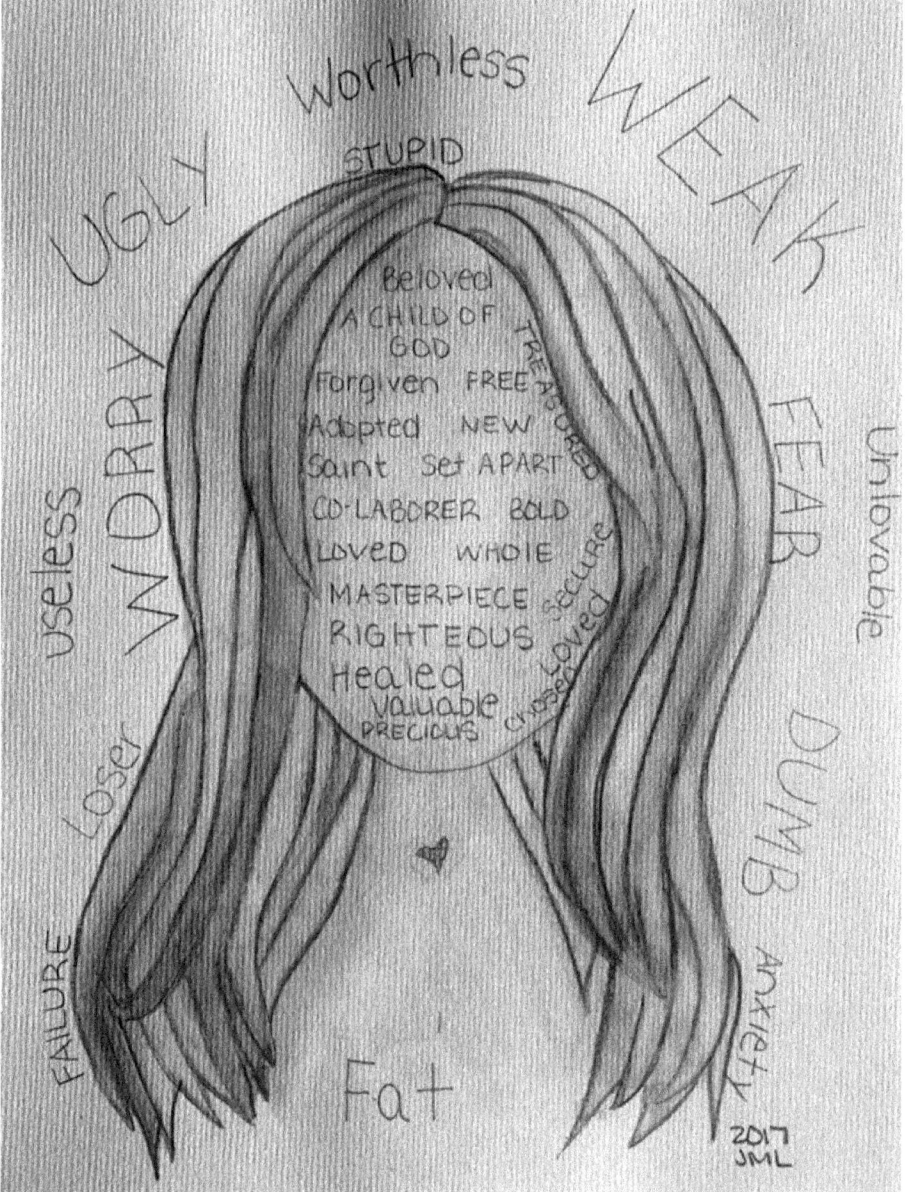

Worthless

WEAK

UGLY

STUPID

WORRY

FEAR

Useless

Unlovable

Beloved
A CHILD OF
GOD
Forgiven FREE
Adopted NEW
Saint SET APART
CO-LABORER BOLD
Loved WHOLE
MASTERPIECE
RIGHTEOUS
Healed
Valuable
PRECIOUS

TREASURED

Secure

Loved
Chosen

Loser

DUMB

FAILURE

anxiety

Fat

2017
JML

JML 23

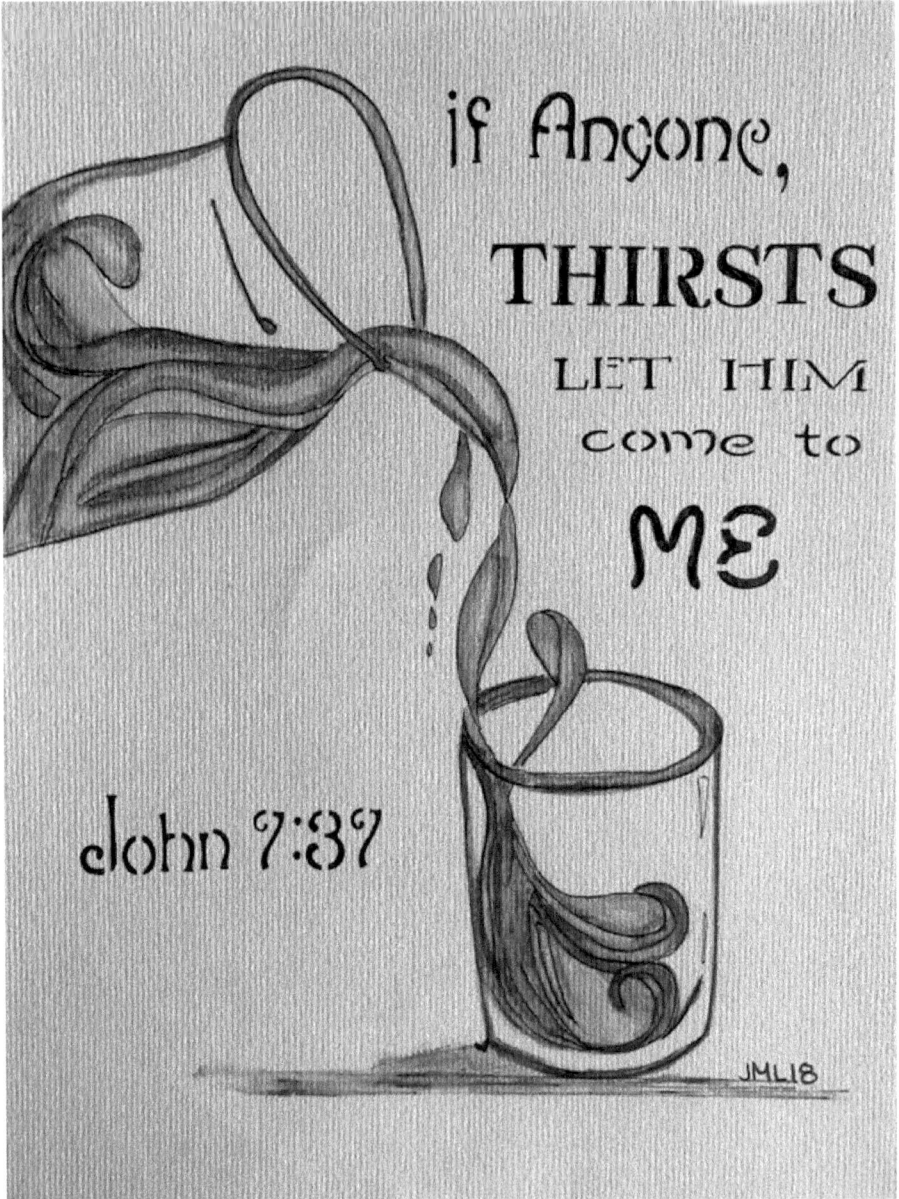

if Anyone,
THIRSTS
LET HIM
come to
ME

John 7:37

JML18

JML22

2021
JML

JML22

JML 23

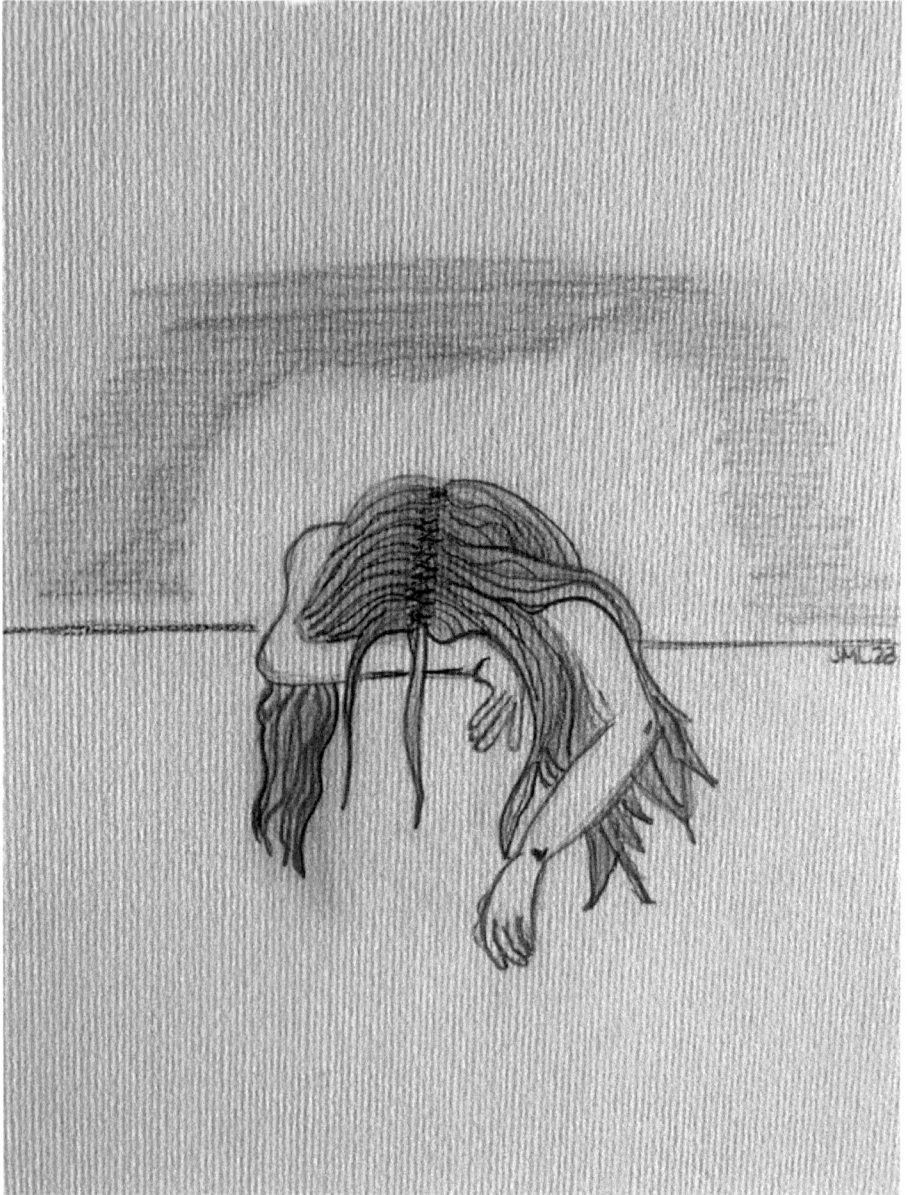

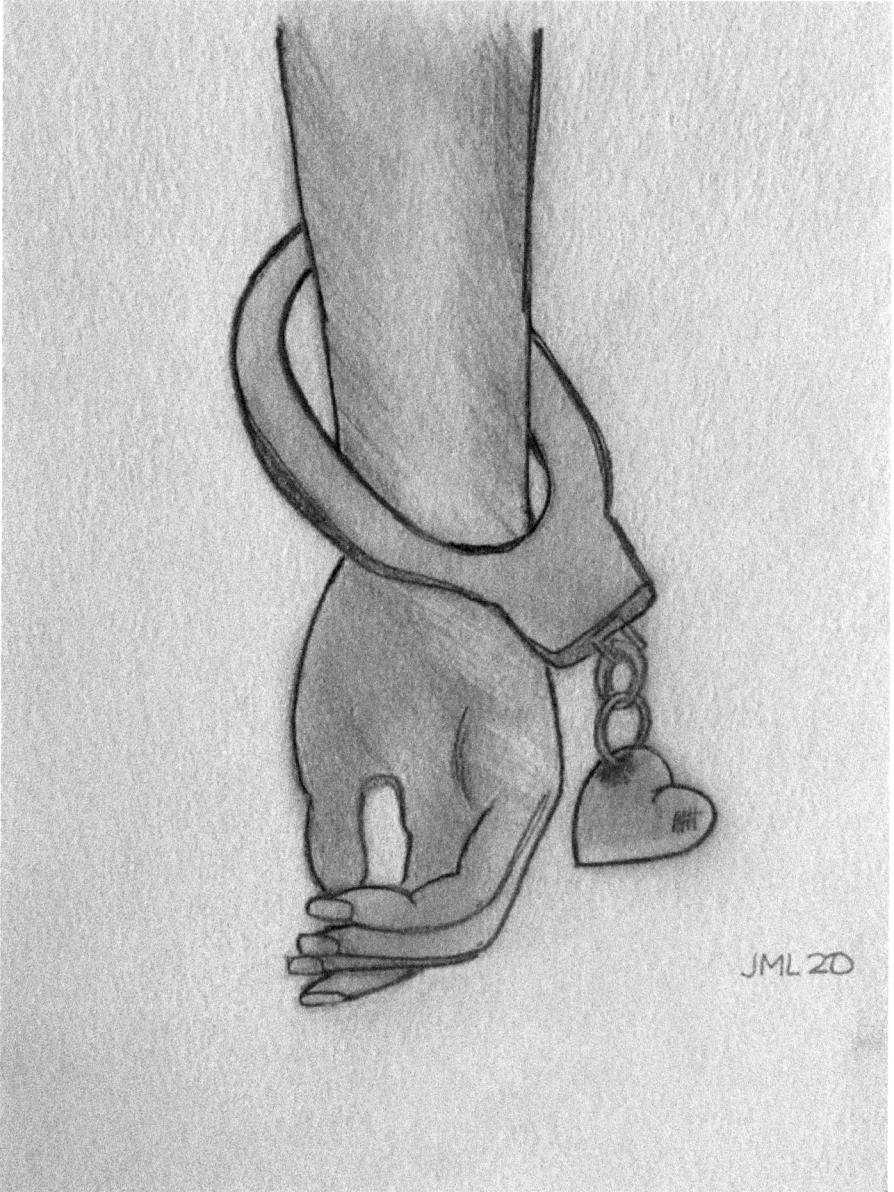

SHE has done a BEAUTIFUL thing — MARK 14

"JML 21"

TEACH US TO NUMBER OUR DAYS

PSALM 90:12

BE
THE
SALT

BE
THE
LIGHT

MATTHEW 5:13-16

Meet Author Jody LaTampa

Jody LaTampa, is devoted Hospice Chaplain and the Co-founder of Revolution Ministries.She has conquered a series of life's most daunting challenges, including adolescent trauma, divorce, single motherhood, and multiple personal losses. Her journey took a remarkable turn when she remarried and co founded Revolution Ministries sharing the gospel and helping those homeless and trapped in addiction.She supported her husband through repeated drug relapses, ultimately taking up his legacy after a tragic overdose claimed his life.

Jody's life story is a remarkable example of the transformative power everyone can find in Jesus. She is dedicated to serving as a source of inspiration for others, demonstrating that even in the face of any adversity, one can find healing, purpose and strength through faith and unwavering trust only found in Jesus.

https://www.facebook.com/RevolutionMinistriesAkron

RevolutionAkron@Yahoo.com

www.ingramcontent.com/pod-product-compliance
Lightning Source LLC
Chambersburg PA
CBHW051940090426
42741CB00008B/1219